ATTITUDE

DETERMINES

ALTITUDE

Our Roller-Coaster Journey Through Stage 4 Cancer

LEO DUGO

with Jessica Brawner

Published by:
Leo Dugo
St. Louis, MO

Some names and identifying details have been changed to protect the privacy of individuals and reader sensitivity. The conversations in the book all come from the author's recollections, though they are not written to represent word-for-word transcripts unless otherwise noted. Rather, the author has retold them in a way that evokes the feeling and meaning what was said and in all instances, the essence of the dialogue is accurate.

ISBN: 978-0-69281-374-4

Cover and interior design: Gary A. Rosenberg

Printed in the United States of America

I dedicate this book to my wife, Debra,
for all the support, strength, and threats
she made if I quit or gave up hope!
I love you, Debra Lou!

INTRODUCTION

I've put this book together to help someone who has been diagnosed with stage 4 colon cancer understand that it *is* possible to live a normal, productive life after treatment—although it's going to be a new normal. This book is a compilation of our CaringBridge Journals. I'm not sure if you ever heard of the CaringBridge website, but it was designed for people who are going through life-and-death illnesses and allows them to communicate with their family and friends over the Internet about their condition and progress. Although I'm not a writer, I found writing these journals to be therapeutic, and the encouraging responses we received from our family and friends helped us beat cancer.

Let me tell you a little bit about myself to get this started: I am a male, seventy-two years old, raised by a loving mom and dad, Florence and Skip. I had a good childhood with my older brother, John, and younger sister, Barbara. I worked forty-one years in the construction industry, mostly in the industrial sector. My hobbies as a kid were baseball, soccer, and golf, and I raced go-karts at the age of fourteen, which inspired me to pursue racing cars for a living: racing sports cars, midgets and sprint cars, stock cars—anything with wheels. It gave me the ambition to drive at the Indy 500, which did not work out because a wall got in the way—literally.

I married a wonderful woman, Debra, in 1973. We have two daughters, Amanda (Mandy) and Jessica, and four grandchildren. Amanda has two adult boys, Dylan and Weston. Jessica has to two younger ones: Truman, a boy, and Remy, a girl. I retired in 2006, whereupon Debra and I embarked on short trips, traveling around in an RV and playing golf wherever we stopped. We did that for six years before deciding to sell the RV and become home-bodies again.

So there you have my life story in a nutshell—that is, up until December 27, 2013, when I was diagnosed with stage 4 rectal colon cancer that metastasized to my lymph nodes, liver, left lung lower lobe and asbestos plaque in both lungs. They said there was no cure; if I did nothing, I had twelve months to live. If I did radiation and chemo, I would have about twenty-four months or more. Bottom line: get your affairs in order, which we did.

It's not exactly what you want to hear to kick off a new year. We have a large circle of family and friends who wanted updates, and our daughter Jessica suggested we do a Caring Bridge Journal online to keep everybody informed on how we were doing and doctor reports as the weeks passed. At first, I was reluctant. One, as I mentioned before, I'm not a writer; two, I'm a bad speller (yeah, spell check); three, my grammar is bad (yeah, Debra and Jessica); and four, I'm bad on the computer. So Jessica took control and set the Caring Bridge account up, so that is where it all started.

However, before I started the Caring Bridge, I sat down and wrote my wife, Debra, a parting letter and cleverly slid it into my life insurance policy so she would find it after I was gone. What I didn't figure was that, when the yearly bill came for the policy, she would put the paid receipt in the policy folder. And guess what? I was still around, so she saw it. So here is the letter. It addresses all my emotions, feelings, and thoughts.

12 to 24

When the doctor tells you, "Don't make any long term trips or plans, you have twelve to twenty-four months to live!" what goes through your mind? Sadness, panic, anxiety, denial, bucket list, relief and how many good days/bad days are ahead of me—that's what went through mine in a matter of a couple of minutes. It is hard, and a lot to comprehend, and hard to act rational with you sitting there beside me. You were so strong, it inspired me to handle this the best way I possibly could. I want to address each of these feelings.

Sadness—I feel so bad I have to leave you. Remember the sundial I bought you years ago with this saying

3

"Grow old with me, the best is yet to be!"? Not so much. However, spending 41-plus years with you have been the happiest years of my life! The day I met you at my mom and dad's house—you were with Barb, Michele, and Baker—I was attracted to you. At first, your young, stunning looks, but the more I got to know you, with your visits to the Willwood house with my sister, Barb, to see my daughter, Mandy, I realized there was more to this young lady then her looks. You had personality, humor and compassion. But never did I think I would have the opportunity to experience you, much less living with and loving you for 41 years. Plus, you became Mandy's mom and raised her. This has been a wonderful adventure with you, so reflect back on all our good times, not what we have to deal with now. I hate leaving you, not being here to take care of you, fixing BIG BREAKFAST, lying next to you, kicking your ass at golf, bowling, jeopardy, Rummikub, and building something for you! You have been everything to me!

Panic—Although I may have seemed calm and in control on the outside, there was panic on the inside. Holy shit, is the will updated? Your pension, your health insurance, life insurance, bank accounts, Weddell, funeral? All the projects I started and had not finished, house maintenance, etc.—manly, take-care-of-business tasks to make this as smooth and painless as possible for you, Mandy, Jessica, Dan, Truman, and Remy?

Denial—This can't be. I feel too good, and they have somebody else's results mixed up with mine.

Anxiety—OK, it is me. How do I fix it and fix it fast? It is like being in a really fast race car but not in the driver's seat, with no control over my destination—not a good feeling for me. I will have to trust others I don't know, prepare for the worst, and expect and work for the best! OH NO! CHEMO! I have said I would not go down the chemo road; I have seen more pain, suffering and more bad days than good days. But hey, that was years ago, when they only had one or two chemo drugs. Now it is different, and it is me. So I will go down the chemo road and fight this. However, if it is not working and the bad days outnumber the good days, it will be time to stop the treatment and live as many good days possible, doing fun stuff together!

God—WOW, where do I start? I know we are pretty close in our beliefs, but I have so many questions I don't think anybody on this earth can answer. I truly believe there is a God and a devil, but who has the most power? If God is in charge, how can he allow children to be born with cancers, deformities, without limbs, or with mental illnesses from the very start? If there is a fair and almighty God, why isn't every child given the same chance to be normal and then make the mistakes we all make at some point? I know there is a lot of good in the world, but there is as much, if not more, bad, but the bad seems to get more press. Maybe that's why there seems to be more bad. What if God is a woman and the devil is a man? Think about that; it would make more sense. Going back in time, it was always the men fighting, killing each other over some stupid shit wars. Don't get me wrong, there are plenty of evil women out there, but I think the men outnumber the women in the evil department. So what is the "hereafter" (time for my punch line: "You know what I'm hereafter")? Who knows? Nobody has come back and said, "Wow, there is a golf course, ball field, race track, etc., in the sky, and we get to pick our favorite age to live forever, doing what we what." Or, "Wow, you should see the hell all you rotten evil people are facing!" Maybe that would end some of this shit. Or maybe this is it. Poof! We are gone, over, toast—who knows? Not I. But I do believe there is a God who created all this. But I'm not sure who is in control. Enough of this; it can be depressing.

Let's talk about you, without me. Deb, you are a beautiful, wonderful, loving, sensual woman, and I would hate if you went into hibernation the rest of your life and become nun-like. There is another man out there that deserves to experience you and make you happy again, but I'm sure he won't compare to me! LOL! Seriously, don't quit living—not saying a man makes life worth living—but start a new adventure. Life was made to live, so please don't shut down. You have always been a good example to our daughters and grandchildren; do so again with my passing. Take your time to mourn, but then move on and enjoy the rest of your life! I will be watching and waiting for you, but if you do choose a new companion, he is not welcome— unless it's a woman. LOL! I love you so much, make the best of what you have left!

I Love You!!!

6∿9

I said that Deb found the letter, but she didn't open it or even mention that she found it. I was in the file looking for something else when I saw that the letter had been moved. I asked her if she wanted me to read it since I had outlived my timeframe. She said yes. We opened a bottle of wine, got a box of Puffs, and snuggled the rest of the night. We went through so many thoughts and emotions as we read and talked about the letter. This is the reason we decided to include this personal letter here. Now, in the pages to follow, we share our Caring Bridge Journals. I say "we" because this was Debra's journey as well as mine. We were in this together.

While I've had my posts corrected for spelling, grammar, and formatting for the purposes of this book (to spare you the task of correcting my spelling and grammar for me!), they accurately reflect the original entries. The majority of the entries are from me. When they are from my daughter, who stepped in for me when I wasn't up to writing, her name will appear along with the entry.

This journal will take you on our roller-coaster ride through all the treatments, the surgeries, and the cure! If you have cancer, we hope that you will *never* give up and keep a good attitude. The medical industry is constantly coming up with new treatments and cures. I am proof of that. Always remember that there is hope, please don't give up! If you are a family member or have a friend that has cancer, stay positive and encourage them to fight for a cure to beat this. If they have a Caring Bridge account offer kind words, thoughts, prayers whatever that will be mentally uplifting. Trust me, it helped me get to this stage.

Now it's time to fasten your seatbelt and enjoy the ride as you travel our roller-coaster of ups, downs, and eventually just ups!

OUR
CARINGBRIDGE
JOURNAL

JANUARY 2014
TO AUGUST 2016

A New Day
January 21, 2014

Several friends suggested I start a journal on this site to keep family and friends updated. After I looked at it, I thought, *Oh, great. I have to set an account up on the computer . . . PANIC!* When I worked at McCarthy, the IT department and several coworkers gave me the name of "Captain Computer," meaning just the opposite. I often managed to screw things up related to the computer. The IT people would draw straws to see who had to come fix my latest screw-up. So our daughter Jessica came to the rescue and set this up for me. Of course, my second journal entry I screwed up . . . go figure. So this is a test journal entry to see if I remember what she taught me last night, and that has been 12 hours ago, so good luck with this.

I think all the radiation side effects are behind me—not that there were a lot, but there were more than I expected. Had a great night's sleep, feel good, BBQ ribs today, get my bowl on (not toilet bowl; we go bowling Sundays), and looking forward to this week of living a normal life!

I will enter a new journal if the doctor has something exciting to tell us this Friday, like, "Oh, my, we got your results mixed up with Leon Dungo!"

See ya.

A Bad Day
January 22, 2014

Well most of you know by now that Deb and I are embarking on a new and exciting adventure: "The Radical Chemo Trip!" We found out on December 31st that I have rectal cancer. (Of all places to get this. I am now officially renaming it "lower colon cancer"! That sounds much better.) Stage 4, spread to lymph nodes, liver, and left lung. Good news: it's not in the bones.

Started five straight days of radiation 1/20 and have one more to go tomorrow. Not much to the radiation. More setting things up than the actual *zap* job they do on me. However, my daughters will be happy and shocked that I now have a tattoo—totally radical, and where you can't see it. We have next week off, then start chemo February 3rd. They put a port in my shoulder for the chemo, they said it would be below the skin, which it is, but thought it would be flush with the skin. Well, it's not; it looks like a mutant bee sting. Actually it looks like a third eye on my chest that got punched and can't open it!

We call BJC West* our new country club; we have been going there daily and everybody knows our name. How exciting. Well enough for the day, to be continued.

Barnes Jewish Christian Hospital

A New Adventure Without the RV
January 24, 2014

Just got my last radiation this morning and rang the BELL! WOO-HOO!

As I was sitting in the waiting room, I got to thinking of all the chemical plants I have worked in since 1964. Many of them had radioactive areas that had a painted line on the ground with signs saying, "Do Not Enter: Radioactive, Material Can Cause Cancer Without Proper Personal Protection!"

When we did work in the radioactive areas, we had to complete a training class and were told how exposure to radiation can cause cancer, so we had to wear special clothing to protect us from radiation. Now here is the weird part: I have cancer, don't know how I got it at this point, but they are treating my cancer with RADIATION, while I'm just wearing a nightgown!? What the . . ? I guess, as the old saying goes, "Fighting fire with fire!"

However, I never see fire pouring out of those fire hoses. Here is some really good news: we have the next ten days off. No treatments, doctors, or country club visits—just life, back to normal and looking forward to it.

Deb and I want to thank everyone for all their kind words, encouragement, thoughts, and prayers. It has helped our outlook moving into the next phase of our adventure.

Chemo Marathon
January 31, 2014

Deb and I met with our oncology doctor today to discuss our chemo cocktail and schedule. WOW. Before this, the only meds I have been taking is an Aleve once in a while for arthritis pain. Now, just for starters, I came home with four meds and get three or four more Monday, not counting the four chemo drugs! I am thinking I might have to get one of those goofy pill organizers I thought I would never need, or want.

So the schedule goes like this: Monday they plug into my port, attach a fanny pack (I hope it matches my shoes) with the chemo and a pump inside, I keep that on for forty-eight hours, and then get unplugged. I then have the next twelve days off to play golf, ski, swim, drive a race car, or lie around to see how I feel. Then the whole process starts again. This will go on indefinitely.

The good news is the radiation is doing its job. The pain and discomfort I have been experiencing is normal for the treatment I had. However, they gave me some new pain meds that REALLY worked, and I feel like new again.

The doctor explained this is a marathon; they can't cure it, but can shrink the tumor and stop the growth from spreading to other areas. The doctor said everybody reacts differently to the side effects of chemo and only time will tell how I will do, but my diet, weight, and exercise program is in my favor to withstand the side effects in a positive way. Except for the hair loss; that *is* going to happen. I only hope I also lose the ear hair and nose hairs, too!

Again, thanks for all the kind words, thoughts, and prayers.

Time to Rally!

By Jessica Brawner
February 4, 2014 • 8:07 pm

Hello! This is Jessica, Leo's daughter, posting on his behalf.

I only run when being chased, so running a marathon has never been a desire of mine. The only way I can imagine myself participating in a marathon would be if I were on the sidelines handing out party favors to the runners as they ran by (runners need party favors, right?), or maybe planning a luncheon for the after party or something equally as fabulous.

The radiation treatment my dad received was a 25-day treatment plan condensed into five powerful, fun-filled days. So the pain from said radiation was twenty-five days' worth of pain, condensed into five fun-filled days, too. We were all caught off guard by this, which we realize seems rather silly in retrospect, but we were too busy cheering each other on and planning the next leg of the race at the time. Add to that the only potential side effects mentioned were "minor fatigue and discomfort." I guess we can file this under one of those "everybody reacts differently to treatments" comments we hear from the doctors. Being vague is the new black in the medical profession; they like to emulate meteorologists with sweeping ranges in their forecasts and blankets of information. My dad has been experiencing major pain. It has been steadily increasing as the days have passed.

I would like to clarify that we really like his team of doctors and have full confidence in them. My comments are a general comedic jab at the nuts and bolts of the marathon we are running and learning.

Even with the pain, in true Leo fashion, he marched into his chemo appointment on Monday ready to fight the good fight. He was sent to the ER instead. The ER is basically a black hole for time, lined with all sorts of fun germs to pick up and take home with you; it's like Disney World, only less expensive. So we spent the day at the ER. They adjusted and changed meds, did some fun scans, poked him a few times, kicked his tires, and sent us home with a new cocktail to help the pain. They did rule out any major "life-threatening issues" with the scan, and they even packed up some extra germs in to-go boxes for us when we left. Such service.

So now the plan is to take medicine A to fix problem B, then medicine B will counteract problem C but might bring on problem D that really wasn't a problem before medicine B was introduced, and, whatever you do, don't expose your skin to the sun on Tuesdays or medicine C might give you hives or make your arm hair grow at a record rate! Wash it all down with Gatorade and increase your fiber and stay away from your old medicine K and you should start to feel better soon. Okay, let's rally again. We can do this!

Fast-forward to this afternoon. I stopped by my parents' house to drop off some groceries and my dad had a low-grade fever and was shaking pretty bad. Now, if you know my dad, you know that the song "The Hippy Hippy Shake" was written all about him. But these were a different brand of shakes. After a call to his doctor, they decided to admit him to the hospital overnight.

He is resting peacefully now and the pain is managed at the moment.

Chemo has been rescheduled for Monday; he needs time to get back in fighting mode before we start that leg of the race. So let the rally begin again.

P.S. If you read this and want to call my mom to support her, please don't say anything too nice to her, or just send her a text; we are running dangerously low on Kleenex at the moment— dangerously low!

We thread humor through our lives a lot; it helps us heal and deal. The truth is, even though things are tough right now, we have an amazing support system and we thank you all for your part in that. It matters and helps tremendously.

Quick Update

By Jessica Brawner
February 6, 2014 • 11:10am

My dad is still in the hospital and will likely be there until tomorrow. They are still working on pain management. Now is not a good time for visitors, but we will update when that has changed.

If you have any fun memories or stories that you want me to pass on to my parents, I am sure they could use a smile.

Thank you all for your kinds words, prayers, and support.

Resting Well

By Jessica Brawner
February 8, 2014 • 7:35pm

My dad must really like it at Chateau Barnes West, because he is still there. Apparently their Jell-O is superb and their hand sanitizer is the softest on hands in town, but really, can it be *that* good? He will likely be there until Monday. We would still appreciate no visitors and will let you know when things have changed.

Home Sweet Home
February 14, 2014

Home at last, home at last, THANK GOD I'M HOME AT LAST!!! Well, the last couple of weeks have been fun and uplifting; however, I feel we are heading in the right direction. We meet today with our oncology doctor to determine if we start chemo Monday, 2/17. I believe we have a good handle on exactly where the pain is that has our adventure in a holding pattern. Deb has been outstanding throughout this whole ordeal as a partner and a nurse. I think she likes me!

Again, thanks for all the comments, thoughts, prayers, and kind words from everyone. By the way, in the guestbook there is a picture attached to the comment from Gail about the playground project. The picture is of our granddaughter, Remy, doing a project with a little boy . . . I want to know, who is this boy?

Ready, Set, Gooooo!!!
February 18, 2014

Yesterday at 9:30 am we started the chemo marathon, and go we did! I'm off and running, but started well behind the pack. By 6:00 pm, I caught the back of the pack and feeling much better than expected. This morning, I'm in the middle of the pack and feeling pretty good. So far, so good.

What amazed me yesterday in the four and a half hours we were there, getting three of our four chemo cocktails, with the forth one (5 FU; what kind of a drug name is that?) in a fanny pack to go, is the amount of people in the waiting room and treatment rooms getting all different types of chemo treatments—young, middle age and old, at just this one cancer treatment center in St. Louis. Just think about how many there are throughout the world! Kind of blew my mind. And that doesn't account for the children's cancer treatment centers. I saw some of the children when we went to Big Barnes Radiation Treatment, which was really heartbreaking. Why target the children with this monster?

I only walked away once, so far, without my stylish fanny pack. I didn't get very far, but sure made a big coffee mess! The fanny pack comes off Wednesday at noon, and the next treatment starts March 3rd. Yahoo!

Hey, Mike, where in the world did you get that go-kart picture dating back to 1962?* They should have made the frames longer back then; no wonder I still get leg cramps! LOL!

Thanks for all the support everyone has shown our family. I can't say enough about Debra and how she has taken great care of me! I think she missed her calling as a nurse.

Mike Miller is our cousin who went to some of our go-kart races to help in the pits and root us on.

Attitude Determines Altitude!
February 20, 2014

My dad was a pilot and he would use the term "Attitude Determines Altitude," meaning the position of the wing flaps would determine the altitude of the aircraft. When I began racing all sorts of go-karts, motorcycles, and cars, he told me this term also applied to everything I would do in life. The better the attitude I had toward whatever I was pursuing in family, life, work, and recreation, the more I could accomplish in whatever I pursued. I found that was true, except in racing when a couple of walls got in my way and ended that dream.

Well, here I am, one and a half days after my first chemo treatment, and I feel pretty good. Actually returned to some routine stuff, like, got out of bed (finally), fed the dog, made coffee, got the paper, stretched for five minutes, and laid back down for a short nap—don't want to overdo! This afternoon we went for a short walk to enjoy the warm weather and sat up most the day.

I am back to my dad's term "Attitude Determines Altitude." I'm feeling better and looking forward to hitting a small bucket of golf balls and bowling this weekend, so if this is the worse it's going to be, I can live with it!

Thanks for all the thoughts and prayers, Deb needs them . . . OK, OK, I do, too.

The Roller Coaster Ride!
February 28, 2014

The best way I can describe this past week is a "roller coaster ride!" And it won't be the next attraction at Six Flags.

This was my week off chemo, and I was expecting some really good days starting last Saturday and getting better day by day. However, I was only getting two or three good hours in a day and there I was, on Wednesday, and I would be starting chemo in four days, which meant I would start this whole chemo process over!

So as pumped up as I was last Saturday, I was slightly deflated to say the least Wednesday night because of feeling so fatigued, the major rash on my body, and the fact that my face looks like I was having a facial skin peel with pimples (these were all expected side effects of the chemo drugs). But lo and behold, I woke up Thursday morning feeling great and I felt great all day and night, and here it is, Friday, and I'm still feeling great.

We had our meeting this morning with our oncology doctor to prepare for Monday's treatment, and he was all excited to see I have a major rash and pimples because it means the chemo drugs are WORKING and doing their job. However, he said the rash will get much worse. I think he was trying to cheer me up. He told us my body is in shock because of the four chemo drugs they are giving me, and it could take three to four sessions before my body acclimates to the drugs and I will start having more and more good days in a row.

So this first session gave me four good days out of fourteen and we will build from there. It just feels SOOOO GOOD to feel good again that I actually went down in my shop and installed new grips on Debra's golf clubs, so now she has no excuse when I whip her butt on the golf course! (I struggled beating her with her old grips, and that's when I felt great, so what am I talking about?) Anyway I am feeling good at this point and looking forward to some warm weather.

A New Mantra!
March 5, 2014

Last Sunday night was our fourth really good day in a row, so we were on a high to do something, but the weather did not cooperate, so we settled in and watched the Academy Awards that night, big whoop-dee-do! My mind was all over the place, trying to process how good I feel and starting chemo tomorrow and how long will it take to start feeling good again. So I was not paying much attention to the awards until they were nominating Best Picture. They were showing a clip from the movie *12 Years a Slave,* and it got my attention. Two slaves that were down and desperate with their situation in life were talking, and the one said, "I DON'T WANT TO SURVIVE, I WANT TO LIVE!" I said to Deb, "OMG, that's what I have been sitting here thinking but couldn't come up with the words." So that, my friends, is my new mantra!

One of my chemo drugs makes me cold, so I always wear a T-shirt. I have a few I call my "Happy Shirts," and they make me smile. You might have seen them; they are the brand Life Is Good. Each has a stick man with a saying, such as the stick man is swinging a golf club that says "Gone Clubbing"; another is a stick man pushing a lawn mower that says "Father Mows Best" (our daughter Mandy appreciates that one), and another has the Grateful Dead logo saying "Grateful Dad" (our daughter Jessica appreciates that one). And my last one: when we adopted our rescue black lab dog, Crazy Betty, they gave us a shirt with a stick dog on it and the caption "Black Dog Club." Betty was free, the shirt $250.00, great deal, huh, but I wouldn't trade her! So now I am having two new shirts made, our Dad's term "Attitude Determines Altitude" and "I Don't Want To Survive, I Want To Live!"

So here we are today, Wednesday, March 5th, and on our SEVENTH good day in a row! Today I will finish up my second chemo treatment at noon, and I feel great. So, my friends, whatever you are doing with all your thoughts, kind words, and prayers, it is working!

A GREAT BIG THANK YOU from Deb and me.

The Indy 500
March 17, 2014

Back in 1951 and 1952, our dad was on the pit crew at the Indy 500. Pete Schmidt, from St. Louis, was the owner of two Indy cars that competed in USAC pavement and dirt tracks throughout the USA. Some of the famous drivers that Pete hired were Sam Hanks, Johnny Parsons, Paul Russo, Jimmy Bryan, Eddie Sachs, and George Tichenor, to name a few.

Dad was also a part owner of a midget open wheel race car that sat in our garage for a year around 1949. I remember sneaking out to the garage and sitting in the cockpit of the race car, pretending I was driving in big races and, of course, winning all of them. I never got to go to Indy to watch back then, but I always got to go to Du Quoin, IL, State Fairgrounds and Springfield, IL, State Fairgrounds for the Indy Dirt Car Races. I was only seven years old but was bitten by the race bug—I wanted to drive one day in the Indy 500!

In 1959, I somehow convinced Mom and Dad to buy me a go-kart and started racing in House Springs, MO, every Sunday. My sister Barbara LOVED going to the races every Sunday too—NOT! As I moved through the different style race cars—SCCA sports cars, motorcycles (that was a really bad idea), midget race cars, and Outlaw Sprints—I kept the Indy 500 dream fresh in my mind and that's where it ended. Deb was nine months pregnant with Jessica, and I broke my neck in a sprint car. The doctor who fixed my neck and my back after a different racing accident said, "It is time to reconsider your racing goals. It has become hazardous to your health and your marriage!" So for once I made the right choice and picked Deb!

So you're probably wondering, is this going anywhere? This morning, Deb and I were walking in our BJC West Country Club, Deb for an eye exam and I for my third chemo treatment—good times on a Monday morning. And there it was, a big flyer in the CC lobby, my dream, my chance to finally compete in the UNDY 5000, March 29th at Forest Park!!! Yes, you read that right—UNDY 5000. It's a Colon Cancer Alliance 5K Race and 1 Mile Fun Walk. And get this: Undy Costume Contest. You can run in your underwear, with your underwear over your outerwear, or with your underwear on your head as a hat. I'm not up for the 5K, but I'm training for the 1-miler just like Du Quoin and Springfield. Not quite exactly how I dreamed of racing at the Indy 500, but you play the cards you're dealt!

Things are going good. Deb and I played 18 holes on Friday; she showed no mercy and beat me on the last hole. We bowled on our league Sunday, and although we are a team, I whipped her butt. I have to take any victory I can get at this stage. This will be a slow three or four days, then I'll be up and running again.

Deb and I appreciate all the kindness and support everyone has shown us.

UNDY 5000 Part 2
March 18, 2014

Several family and friends requested more information about joining Deb and me on the UNDY 5000, so here is the scoop: To register, go to the website www.undy5000.org; the site has all the details you will need. All the proceeds go to the research and development to find a cure for cancer. I registered Deb and myself under the team name "Dugo Squadrae," long story short, which is Italian for "Dugo Team." It was something Dad would paint on the race cars. You can click on and join our team.

Oh yeah, Jimmy, I asked your undy question. They said undies were optional, but make sure your kilt is long enough; they only want to see your bagpipes!*

After the walk/run, Deb and I would like to invite all our fellow walkers, bagpipers, and rooters back to our house for BBQ brats, dogs, drinks, laughs, and fun!

Any questions? Give us a call.

Jimmy plays the bagpipes in a Hibernian order and wanted to dress in full attire with a kilt.

New Things Learned
April 1, 2014

Sunday was the UNDY 5000 Run/Walk, and we had twenty-eight family and friends, including our six-year-old grandson Truman and 4 year old granddaughter Remy, join Deb and I for the walk. It was cold and windy, the worst part was waiting around for an hour before they dropped the green flag to start the run. Once we started everybody got warmed up and finished in fine form, instead of a finish line they had a GIANT COLON we walked through with all the things that can go wrong visible and named, enlighten and CREEPY! The attached awesome photo collage of the event was created by my brother and sister-in-law John and Jan, I think you will notice a man in white long johns with purple thong underwear on the outside keep trying to join our party telling us he is our cousin. We kept moving away from him till he showed us his ID, he IS our cousin Mike Miller from Springfield, IL and brought his whole family including a dog for the run, and the dog would not go near him! They had a Costume Contest at the event and no, Mike did not win (go figure), however our daughter Mandy and her two girlfriends Jennie, Samantha, and her dog Libby Borden did win, all decked out with tutus—really cute! After the run, we all went back to our house for BBQ, drinks, and laughs. It was a great day, and it was the largest turn out for the Colon Cancer Undy 5000 in the U.S., earning over $180,000.

New Lesson Learned #1: Colon cancer is the MOST curable cancer if caught early! And they do that with a regular scheduled colonoscopy. As I mentioned before, I had one ten years ago at age fifty-nine and all was good, and they said come back in ten years for another. Well, this is my tenth year, so that didn't work out as expected. Here is the thing: as I aged, there continued to be new aches and pains that a couple of Advils fixed, so I didn't think much of different changes with my body. So here is what I have learned and will share: If you have a change in your bowl movements and you experience any bleeding, GO SEE YOUR DOCTOR to make sure it is nothing, or something they can fix! Plus, if any of your immediate family has or has had colon cancer, your doctor needs to know and set you up for routine examines because it is hereditary. PLEASE, PLEASE do this; you don't want to go through what we are going through!

New Lesson Learned #2: I noticed in the last few years that my memory recall is not what it used to be, like walking into a room with a purpose or to get something, only to realize I forgot what I came in the room for! Well, in the last two months I've been getting worse; I get up to get something, but I don't always get to the room or I forget what room I need to go to. I talked to our doctor about this, and he said I am experiencing "chemo brain"! CHEMO BRAIN? SERIOUSLY, CHEMO BRAIN? What the . . . ? Just what I need. However, I can now use it when Deb asks me why I didn't take the trash out like she asked—CHEMO BRAIN! How come I left the toilet seat up? CHEMO BRAIN! You get the picture. It might not be so bad after all.

New Lesson Learned #3: Actually, this is not a new lesson, but something we have known for a long time. Without loving caring family and friends, this journey would be really, really tough and at times unbearable! Deb and I have been strong for each other, but the times we struggle, it always seems like we get what we need to help lift us up from all of you. And it boggles our mind how you know what we need when we need it! Amazing!*

Actually we are doing really good; my strength is slowly coming back, I'm gaining weight back, and we are doing more and more normal things. In fact, we went out Friday, 3/21, and played 9 holes. It wasn't pretty until the 6th hole. I got a hole in one, and I needed it to beat Deb— YES! However, Deb reminded me as I was gloating that she has 4 hole in ones and still in the lead in that category. Talk about raining on my parade.

We started our fourth chemo treatment this week, and we got some good news from our oncology doctor: We get a CT scan next week to see how much the tumors have changed. Depending on the changes, they will change the chemo drugs, hopefully lessening the dosage. We will get a

---

If your support system isn't as strong as you would like, please find a support group. There are support groups for every type of cancer, and they will help you through these trying times.

one- or two-month chemo break about four to six months from now, which really makes us happy and gave us something big to look forward to. I keep singing one verse of this old Huey Lewis song in my head. It goes like this: "I want a new drug . . . that won't keep me up all night . . . won't make my face break out . . . won't make my hair fall out!" That last one I added, and I don't think Huey was singing about the chemo drug.

Again, Deb and I thank all of you for your thoughts and prayers, and for just being our family and friends!

Chemo Break
April 11, 2014

The last two weeks have been rough. To give you an idea of "rough," without too many details, this past Tuesday was my worst day since this started. I'll leave it at that.

So Wednesday morning, I woke up with a new attitude that "yesterday is over and today is a fresh start." While flossing my teeth, something popped out of my mouth, fell into my sleeve and rolled down to my elbow. I thought, *What the . . . ?* I straightened my arm out, and out of my sleeve popped a TOOTH! Not just a tooth, but a complete tooth with the root and my crown attached.* Luckily, it fell right into my hand. Unluckily, my hand was over the sink, so I carefully moved to the side of the sink and attempted to place it on the vanity when it popped out of my hand, bounced around on the vanity, bounced against the wall, and dropped into the little crack between the wall and the vanity, out of reach and out of sight. %#@$&!

After an hour of bending wires in various shapes to fish the tooth out, removing all the vanity drawers, and removing the base molding, I finally got the tooth out. Our dentist

---

The chemo side effect that causes mouth sores and dry mouth can also cause funny things to happen to your teeth—which are not so funny!

got me in right away, only to tell me he can't use the tooth; he threw it away and will make me a new one. Now I wish I'd kept the tooth and had it mounted like a fish because it put up such a good fight!

This past Thursday—yesterday—was our first good day since our last chemo treatment, so I am not looking forward to starting the next chemo this coming Monday. I also had my CT scan yesterday and met with our oncology doctor today, and we were ready for some good news. And good news is what we got! The report showed the chemo is working; the tumors in the colon, lymph nodes, liver, and lung have slightly shrunk! The doctor gave us a two-week chemo break to let my body heal and get my mojo back. As they say "Just what the doctor ordered" and, brother, were we happy to hear that.

On top of that, they are going to reduce the amount of chemo to lessen the side effects I have been struggling with, which should start giving us more good days between treatments. Deb and I are going to kick back, relax, play some golf, and enjoy the next two weeks.

Again, thanks for all the thoughts, prayers, and kind words.

Break Over, Back to Work!
April 29, 2014

Our two-week chemo break was great; my body, fingers, and mouth healed and the rash is all but gone! This was the best two weeks we have had since January, and I got my mojo back, along with some strength. I did a few projects around the house; it felt great to be productive again. I also started a project at The Quarry Golf Course before this all started, but never finished it, so I decide to "get 'er done," and our daughter Mandy jumped in to help. We knocked a four-hour job out in two hours and still had the time and energy for 9 holes, in which Deb and Mandy managed to beat me. They showed no mercy on me!

Chemo Happy Hour!
May 12, 2014

OK, so I'm really stretching it. It's Monday morning, and I'm sitting here at our BJC country club getting pumped up with my new and improved chemo treatment. Yes, you heard that right, another new chemo cocktail! Ummm, and it is good!

Our paper delivery person must be having car trouble; for the last two days, the paper has been late. We start our mornings off reading the paper with our breakfast, so this morning I read our new AARP paper instead. When I read the paper, I skim through all the story headings looking for good and uplifting stories, so it does not take long to get to the sports and funny pages, which are the best part. Oh, I also check the obituaries to make sure I'm not in them. So far, so good!

Well, the AARP was not the good and uplifting experience I was looking for. Holy smokes, some of the stories were "Planning Your Exit Strategy" or "Last Letters From Fallen Heroes That Lost Their Lives"—a real tear jerker. "Alzheimer's Test One in Nine over 65 Have It" . . . my mom and dad had it—oh good! If I get this, too, I won't know I have cancer; that could be a positive! And there were plenty of other real story downers, so I went and watched Mickey Mouse Clubhouse on TV and drank my honey-laced tea and watched Goofy be goofy.

We had a really good weekend, starting Friday. We played golf at the Quarry, and Deb got an eagle on the par 4, 13th hole. She hit a perfect drive and a perfect 129 yard second shot in the hole. However, I finally beat her.

Saturday was our granddaughter, Remy's fifth birthday party. At the party, they had a magician who was really good and funny that had us all—the kids and adults—laughing, but my favorite part was just watching all the little five- and six-year-olds running around the yard, playing like in the old days instead of sitting in front of a screen like zombies. Oh, yeah, the food, drink, and visiting with all the family and friends were really good, too.

Sunday was Mother's Day, and it was a beautiful day. We played golf with our daughter Mandy and her friend Joe. It was a challenge match, girls against the guys. Although it was Mother's Day and the girls always rule, it did not happen Sunday, but it did go until the 17th hole to shut them up! (That will be the day, when I shut them two up.)

Well, my three chemo drugs are almost finished up and they will hook the fanny pack pump up with my fourth chemo 5FU drug and send me home and back Wednesday to have the pump removed. I'm about out of things to say, so I'm outta here.

We are looking forward to a fun-filled summer of activities. Hope you are, too!

The Good, the Bad & the Better
May 27, 2014

Well, here we are at our BJC country cub, waiting to get pumped up. Because of the Memorial Day holiday, the nurse said today will be crazy because they will have Monday and Tuesday patients coming in for their chemo cocktail—all seventy-five patients, a new single day record at BJC CC. I'm so happy and proud to be a part of the new record, being I stunk up the Senior Olympics Golf and Bowling events this weekend.

With that, I'll explain the "Good, the Bad & the Better" title of this post, like the movie. I could have used *Ugly* where I used *Better,* but I didn't want to have two negatives; one is enough!

Chemo Treatment:

Good—Two weeks ago, they reduced my chemo treatment and the first part of that week was better than before; I only had both thumbs split open, instead of all ten fingers.*

Bad—The other side effects got worse. I only had three good days out of the last fourteen, and that is not enough for me, and the doctor agreed. The chemo is staying in my system longer and fighting the good fight, though, so I guess that should be in the better column?

Another "lovely" chemo side effect.

Better—They are changing me from a fourteen-day chemo treatment schedule to a twenty-one-day schedule, meaning I get an extra week to recover and heal. HOORAY!!!

Senior Olympics Weekend:

Good—Friday was the first day I felt good, and I played in the 9-hole Senior Olympics Golf Tournament. The flights are divided by age groups, so I was in the 65–70 group, but was riding and playing with my good friend Bob Sido. I have to tell you, Bob is ninety-three, but you would not guess it, and he played really good. We played with two other gentlemen, both named Tom. One Tom was eight-three and the other Tom was eighty-five, so I was the good eyes of our group.

Bad—I started the first hole, a par 4, by driving my tee shot out of bounds, re-teeing another ball, and hitting a tree about 100 yards from the tee box. So you know where this is going—from bad to ugly! I got to watch all our group's good shots and help them find their balls. Too bad they had to watch all my bad shots and nobody found my balls.

Better—Bob won the gold medal (plastic) in his flight, Tom 85 won gold, and Tom 83 won silver. All three whipped my butt, and there were too many in my flight for me to even bring a ribbon home, but I was really happy to spend the morning with my friend Bob, getting some exercise, and enjoying the day.

Senior Olympics Bowling:

Good—Deb was teamed with our good friend Patty Myers, and they are the defending champions for 2011, 2012, and 2013 in the women's division. I won't say the age group, but they were the youths of all the contestants. Dave Seithel, my best friend and best man in our wedding forty-one years ago, was my partner for the last three years, and we too are the 2011, 2012, and 2013 defending champions. However, we think we outlived the competition.

Bad—The bowling alley's air condition units were broken, which caused a lot of humidity, which caused all the approaches, and especially at the foul lines, to get very sticky so you could not slide. Now picture this: They have about fifty senior citizens, ages between 50 and 100, stumbling and tripping every time they throw the ball, a good setting for a commercial—"Help I have fallen and I can't get up!" Thank goodness nobody got hurt, but a lot of grumbling was heard. Go figure, old crabby people; that doesn't happen often.

Better—I think Deb and Pat still won the gold medal. However, Dave and I really stunk the gutters up, and the only way we would have won anything is if our competition had died at the foul line! But the better part came afterward; we went back to our house for drinks, BBQ, and a lot of laughs.

Final Thoughts:

All in all, we are doing pretty good. This was a great weekend! Friday golf with Bob; Saturday golf with Deb and BBQ at Paulette and Larry's, along with Cathy and Mike; Sunday bowling and BBQ with Patty, Sandy, and Dave; Monday golf with Deb, Mandy, and Joe; then BBQ with Mandy, Joe, Jessica, Dan, Truman, and Remy. Don't get any better than that. Like my shirts say, "Life Is Good!"

Deb and I are looking forward to our next three weeks before the next chemo starts. Thanks for all of your support; it means a lot to Deb and me. Well, I am about out of things to say, so I am out of here.

21-Day Salute
June 19, 2014

The last three weeks completed my first twenty-one days between chemo treatments, and all went well—actually, it was a lot better. I still had all the side effects and they continued throughout the three weeks without any pattern, but all in all, I had more good days than the fourteen-day schedule they had me on.

Now the real test will be next week to see if we can stay on the twenty-one-day schedule. I will have a CT scan Tuesday and meet with our doctor Thursday to get the CT results and talk about treatment options and schedules.

Three weeks ago, Deb said she thought she saw a mouse in the garage, so I went to the hardware store to buy a mouse trap. Well, you've always heard the phrase "Trying to build a better mouse trap." They did, or at least they thought they did. There on the shelf, right before my eyes, was "The Better, Improved Mouse Trap!" It was a plastic clam shell mouse trap, boasting that you won't get your fingers caught in the trap trying to bait it—which was true—and you don't have to touch the little stinker when you catch one because you just squeeze the back of the clam shell to release the mouse. I believe that would have been true if I would have caught a mouse with this New and Improved Mouse Trap! You see, I fed the mouse for one week trying to catch it. The little stinker must have been the one who invented it, and it was a mouse feeder not a trap.

So I went back to the hardware store and bought two good old, reliable, wooden Victor mouse traps. In the last two weeks, I have caught NINE mice that have been living in our garage for who knows how long. NINE . . . CREEPY!

Last week was quite a test for my buddy Bob Sido and me. Bob invites me each year to play in his Member Guest Golf Tournament. It is a three-day golf tournament, with 18 holes on Thursday, 27 holes on Friday, and 18 holes on Saturday. You have to realize Bob is ninety-three and had back surgery this past winter, and I was all lathered up with sunscreen, bug repellent, and a big brimmed hat that made me look like I was off to a safari, rather than a golf tournament. We played five matches in our flight, and our goal was not to get shut out and lose all the matches. Thanks to Bob's spectacular play, we almost won our flight; had I sunk a 4-foot putt on the last hole we would have won!

All in all, things are going well and we are anxious to see what the doctor says next week. Until then, we will catch you later.

New Ideas, New Decisions!
July 7, 2014

Got my CT and met with our oncology doctor last week and got a good report! Nothing is growing any bigger, and in several areas, there are signs the cancer is shrinking. Our doctor just got back from an oncology conference where they discuss new ideas, new drugs, and new treatments, and he wanted to share some of the new ideas and proposed a new approach for us to consider. They have been removing the tumor that metastasized in patients with stage 4 cancer, which then stops sending the seeds out that causes the spreading. Then they treat the other areas, hoping to bring the cancer into remission.

That sounds pretty good and reasonable, except for the "hoping" part. There are no guarantees that this will work in all patients or what the success percentage there is because it is a brand new treatment. The other part that I'm not too excited about is, because of where the tumor is, they would have to remove my lower colon area. I would then have to have a colostomy bag for the rest of my life. I know, I know, there are a lot of people who live a normal life with a bag. I'm just not excited about having my plumbing on the outside. So tonight I am going to a colostomy support group to see what I can learn.*

Another concern is that my oncology doctor wants me to return to the fourteen-day chemo schedule, instead of the twenty-one-day schedule we just completed, because he was concerned the chemo would be out of my system and I would not be protected the third week. However, we compromised, and we stayed on the twenty-one-day schedule and he added a 5FU chemo boost. Oh boy, I can't wait to see what that will bring!

So from what I understand about this surgical procedure, the normal recovery time after this surgery is six to eight weeks for someone without cancer, so I don't know if mine would take longer. Even so, I could not have chemo throughout the surgery or recovery period. Now my question is, while I am without chemo for about six to ten weeks, what is happening to the cancer in my lymph nodes, liver, and lungs during this period? My fear is they will be having a BIG party and spread the word: No more chemo!

They also can't say how much longer this will add to my overall time and the quality of life this can bring; it's all a gamble. The other thing is, when they originally found the cancer, the surgeon said it was inoperable, so our oncology doctor is talking to our surgeon and will then set a meeting up with that surgeon and us. Well, that's a lot to think about and consider.

Keep in mind that not all colon cancers require surgery and a colostomy bag. The earlier they catch it, the better chance of treating it without surgery. Don't skip your routine colonoscopy; this is the best way to stay on top of it. If it runs in your family, let your doctor know.

First, I don't like surgery. (Who does?)

Second, I don't want to be a lab rat. (Who would?)

Third, I don't like the thought of having my plumbing on the outside. (Maybe a plumber would—it would be an easy fix if something was stopped up, broke, or leaky . . . yuck!)

Fourth, I don't like to think about how long and how many good days we will lose during recovery from the surgery, and whether will we make those up or whether it will just be a wash.

I know, that's a lot of negatives I just listed. But I think they are valid, so now I'll list the positives:

First, this could produce a longer life, which means I can watch our family grow up and not miss anything.

Second, there's a possibility of getting the other cancer into remission, which means no more chemo.

So there you go. We have a lot of research and decisions to make, but we are going to take our time, ask a lot of questions and make our decision this late fall or early winter. Right now, we are doing great. I'm feeling really good. I finished some wood working projects, and I'm playing more golf than before. Again, Deb and I thank everyone for all your thoughts and prayers; it means a lot to us.

To Be, or Not to Be?
July 28, 2014

That is the question, or instead of "Be," it should be "Surgery."

Last Thursday, I had the MRI from HELL! I was in the little tube for an hour and a half while they took pictures, all the time smiling for those pictures. Actually, to amuse myself and to pass the time away, I closed my eyes and started playing the Ann Briar Golf Course in my mind, shooting the best round in my life. Wow, what an imagination!

However, on the 18th hole I was thinking this should be about over—the MRI, that is—and at the same time, the MRI tech said, "OK, we only have two more pictures to take with the breathing commands and then you can relax and breathe normally for the next twenty minutes!"

"REALLY? 20 MORE MINUTES? I'm hot, my arms are rubbing on the sides of the tube every time they move the sled back and forth (every 30 seconds), my back is hurting from being in this position for the last 70 minutes, and I just shot the best round of (pretend) golf, and the tube seems to be getting smaller. And you want me to relax and breathe normally for 20 minutes? OK, no problem, I'll just keep smiling and—oh, by the way, the music and the fan quit working!"

She said, "Yes, we are working on that." However, neither one came back on.

Friday we met with our oncology doctor to discuss the surgery option and my meeting coming up next Friday with a new surgeon he wants me to see. I started our meeting expressing no more than 5FU chemo boost, because it kicked my butt for two straight weeks, and he agreed. Then we told him our fears of being off chemo for two to three months and the lymph nodes go on a road trip, spreading cancer like Johnny Appleseed. He listened to all our concerns, and then it was his turn. He said only 20% of patients with stage 4 rectal colon cancer would qualify for this procedure, and because of the way my cancer has responded to the chemo, I would be in the top 20%. How cool—I always wanted to be in the top percent of something.

However, that doesn't mean I will qualify. The surgeon we meet next Friday will determine that from the MRI we just took. You see, he is the liver surgeon, and if there is enough good liver without cancer, he can remove the bad part along with the lymph nodes, and then the lung surgeon can remove the lower lobe of the left lung at the same time the colon surgeon will be removing my rectum, colon, and tumor, all in one day. Then, after I recover, approximately six to eight weeks later, we start chemo again every fourteen days for the next six months to get any cancer that might be hiding. Then I "should" be cancer-free and no more chemo! That is, unless something that was in a really good hiding spot shows up down the road. Then maybe I'll need another operation and chemo.

HMMMM . . . let me take a moment to digest all of this and try to make an intelligent decision. It sounds like I'll be going to Dobbs Auto Care instead of BJC—"In, Up, Fix, Out!"—but without a warranty.

Honestly, the thought of being cancer-free and no more chemo sounds great, but getting to that point seems painfully long and no fun at all. So we will meet with the liver surgeon next Friday, 8/1, to see what he says. I may not qualify for the surgery, which would make the choice for me, and that would be OK with me. We are going into this with an open mind. However, I'm 95% against having all these parts removed.

I am currently at our country club getting the Chemo Club Special, but it will not take as long because they have adjusted my cocktail again and eliminated the one chemo that has made my fingers and toes numb.* I was amazed how much balance you lose when you can't feel your toes. Deb thought I was drinking too much, as I would stumble around and lose my balance. If I would have had to walk the white line for a police officer, I would have been in trouble.

They will be hooking me up to my 5FU pump shortly and we will be out of here, so keep the faith and hang in there! Enjoy each day as it comes and don't look back!

---

*This is another "fun little" chemo side effect.

The Liver Doctor
August 1, 2014

Here is the scoop in a nutshell:

They want me to complete two more chemo sessions, fourteen days apart, then another MRI (from Hell) and CAT scan, then another meeting with the team of doctors to discuss surgery. All the doctors feel I'm a top candidate for this procedure and will recover 90% to 100%, so that's a plus.

The cancer has shrunk in all areas, so the chemo is doing the job—another plus.

They would not have to remove any part of my liver, but cut the larger spots out and burn the smaller ones (the larger ones were the size of a quarter, but now have shrunk). Another plus.

They would remove my rectum and colon with the main tumor and install a colostomy bag. That's a minus.

They would not do anything to the lungs at this point; it would be too much to add on in one operation. But the spots on the lung are all but gone, so maybe nothing would be required later because of the chemo, but nothing can be done about the asbestos plaguing.* Plus and minus.

If we decide to go forward with the surgery, it won't happen till October or November because I have to be off chemo for four to six weeks before surgery. Recovery from surgery will be six to eight weeks, because this is a "BIG" surgery. "BIG" was the word they used—not exactly what I wanted to hear.

If I just stay on chemo without surgery, history shows the cancer becomes resistant to the chemo in twelve to sixteen months and no longer works. I feel maybe we can rewrite history and go longer. However, I'm not a doctor. OK, that was a pretty big nutshell!

Lots to think about, and we have time to figure this out. However, I am more open to this approach than I was two hours ago.

Our thanks to all our family and friends that have been so supportive throughout this ordeal.

I thought I knew all the bad things you can get from asbestos, but the plaguing was new to me. They said it was like scar tissue on the lining of my lungs—lucky me.

A Race for a Cure!
August 25, 2014

We met with our oncology doctor last Friday, and after many sleepless nights and serious soul searching, we decided to do the surgery. It was not an easy decision. However, it was the only one that offered us a cure. And that was the key and selling word: CURE!

You may think, *So why would that be such a hard decision?* OK, so I'm a Big Baby about being sliced and diced on. But there was more to it than that, you see. There is a real chance they can't get everything for fear some little stinkers are hiding somewhere else in my body.

After a long discussion with our doctor about the procedure and preparation and timing, we learned the following:

- Today will be our last chemo treatment before surgery. Yeah!

- Two weeks after this chemo treatment, I get another MRI (from HELL, boo!), a PET scan, and a chest x-ray.

- Depending on the above test, especially the PET Scan, the doctors will determine if they can operate or not. The PET Scan will show if there is any cancer anywhere else in my body and, if so, how large an area the additional cancer covers. This may cause the surgery to be canceled and put me back on the fourteen-day chemo schedule. Ugh!

- If surgery is a go, I will be off chemo for three to four weeks before surgery. Yeah!

- After surgery, I will be in the hospital for two to three weeks and in recovery for four to six weeks. During surgery, they will put an infusion pump in my side that will feed chemo directly into the liver for six months after recovery, and then I'm CURED! Woo-hoo!

However, the doctor said there is no guarantee that cancer won't pop its ugly head up down the road. If that happens, we will deal with it at that time, but until then, we are feeling good and looking forward to the CURE and living a long life!

My preparation for the surgery includes increasing my exercise program and increasing my food intake to fatten myself up for the surgery. I now have to buy some big boy pants!

Thanks again for all your comments, thoughts, and prayers.

Surgery Bound!
September 18, 2014

Had our PET scan and MRI, and met with our liver surgeon and anesthesiology team this week and everything is a GO! We meet with our colon surgeon next Thursday, and we have lots of questions to be answered.

The surgery will take place within the next three weeks, but we don't have a date yet, so we are going to squeeze as much fun as possible into this time frame before the surgery.

The surgery will be at Big Barnes downtown, and they are guessing a two- to three-week stay at the hospital, then home to heal and work on my golf swing. I really need to work hard on my swing, being as Deb just got her fifth hole in one last week, and she keeps reminding my how many she has.

We are really excited that the surgery is a go and that we have a chance for a cure. However, I have to admit that I'm a little nervous about being cut on and having lots of parts removed—and who wouldn't be? However, I plan on beating all the doctors' expectations with a shorter recovery time and being back to doing everything by March 2015.

Our family has always been close, but the thing that really surprises me is how much closer this has made us. Really, Deb is like joined at the hip to me. Wherever I go, Deb goes, and I'm not complaining. It's just amazing!

I don't think woman was made from one of man's ribs. I think it was the hip bone!

Well, I'm off to have some fun and cut the grass. I had to add a second seat on the lawn mower for Deb.

When we get a surgery date, we will update this site. Again, thanks for all your comments, encouragements, and prayers.

Reality Check!
September 26, 2014

So what got us to this stage of the game was a chance for a cure. We met with our colon surgeon Thursday, and he didn't sugarcoat anything, and we wanted it that way. It was a really good meeting, but not exactly what we expected or wanted to hear. The truth is sometimes hard to swallow.

He explained the operation in great detail (scary!), emphasized how serious this operation was, and gave us several options to consider, being as the liver cancer will be the one that will finally get me sometime down the road. Don't know if it's a long road trip or a short one.

Option 1: Being as I have responded so well to the chemo, I can stay on the chemo treatment we are on and keep a close watch for any growth or shrinkage.

Option 2: Being as I'm not crazy about having a colostomy bag, I can do only the liver surgery and have the infusion pump installed directly to the liver. However, that's not a cure; it only extends my life for who knows how long, because the colon tumor is still there, waiting to spring into action after it builds a resistance to the chemo and starts sending its seeds out again. I would still have to do chemo from both the infusion and my power port. Oh boy, double chemo but no colostomy bag! We would keep an eye on the tumor, and if there was a change or new growth, we would have to decide to have the colon operation and the bag installed. UGH! A second operation is not what I want, but who would?

Option 3: Have the BIG SCARY operation that is scheduled for September 30 and HOPE it's the CURE!

I say "hope" because I asked him how many cases like mine have been documented and successfully cured? The answer was none. So trying to look on the bright side, I could be the FIRST to be CURED! It's always good to be first, unless you're on the front line going into a war.

We asked him, if I was his dad what he would suggest? He could not answer. Apparently I am the talk of the BJC oncology, colon, and liver team that has been discussing our case and looking at our options. And the team is divided on which way to go.

One good note was my hospital stay may only be a week long. YEAH!

We met with our liver surgeon today to get his take on our situation. He started out by saying there is no right or wrong decision on which way to go, and again we talked about all the options, then decided to go for the BIG SCARY operation and get the damn tumor out of my body so it's not always on our minds and thinking of a sneak attack down the road.

I will have an infusion pump on my left side, colostomy bag on my right side, and a power port in my chest! I know what I want for my birthday: a saddle bag for all my body stuff.

So Tuesday, September 30th, we are off to BJC for the CURE!

Looking back now from September 30, 2014 to the time of this writing, it has been over 24 months since we chose the BIG SCARY OPERATION. As tough a decision as that was, it was the right one. My next entry wouldn't be for another two weeks. I had no choice but to take a break from my journal during this time. It was a wait-see-and-hopefully-recover period. The amount of support we received from family and friends continued to pour in, and my hope was to be back at my computer soon with a good report.

I Got Knocked Down, But I Got Up Again!
October 16, 2014

For those of you who have not heard that song, that's pretty much how I have felt the last couple of weeks, but I'm on the mend. When they told me this would be a big operation, I thought, *OK, how much bigger could this be compared to the back surgery or the neck surgery I have had in the past?* The answer is WAY BIGGER!

However, they removed the cancerous tumor that has been spreading all the bad seeds throughout my body, along with several other parts that I apparently don't need to live a normal life, whatever that may be from here out.

Nurse Debbie has been taking really good care of me, along with getting the whip out (I like it when she puts her tall boots on with the whip). She has me walking about one mile a day, which makes me feel better every day. We see our oncology doctor tomorrow to discuss the operation and when we start chemo up again. I'm thinking maybe this coming Monday, and if so, I will be finished with all the chemo treatments in April or May 2015! At that point, I will have all the pumps and ports removed and start living life again. WOO-HOO!!!

Sitting upright is still a problem, and I have just maxed out my sitting upright limit, so again, thanks for all your support, thoughts, prayers, and kind notes.

Off to the RACES!!!
November 3, 2014

Back in the sixties, there was a racetrack in Wentzville, MO, called the Mid America Raceway, or MAR. They would advertise on the radio, and a deep voiced man would shout, "SUNDAY, SUNDAY, SUNDAY, BE THERE AT MAR WHERE THE BIG ONES ARE! SEE THEM EXPLODE OFF THE STARTING LINE! Blah, blah, blah!!!"

Today I start my six-month chemo race, and if I had to rewrite that ad, it would go like this: "MONDAY, MONDAY, MONDAY, BE THERE AT BJC RACEWAY! SEE HIM EXPLODE OFF THE STARTING LINE WITH NEW DUAL-CHEMO INTAKES AND A NEW TUNED EXHAUST SYSTEM!"

Actually, we are excited to get the chemo started—not that I'm excited about getting chemo, but the sooner I start, the sooner I'll be finished. The game plan is six months of chemo with a treatment every two weeks, so if everything goes as planned, I will be finished the end of April 2015. I like the sound of that.

Also, we just found out they are taking me off the chemo that has caused the neuropathy* in my feet and hands, and they're switching it for a chemo that will make my hair fall out. I am really excited about this. I will gladly give up my hair to get the feeling back in my hands and feet and gain my balance back. YEAH! Of course, the feet and hand feelings will take at least a year to heal.

My dear sister-in-law, Denise, got me a shirt for my birthday with the saying, "No Colon and Still Rolling." I had a meeting with my colon surgeon last week, and I wore the shirt. He loved it and had his nurse take a picture of him and me, arm in arm. I'm not sure what he will do with it . . . but maybe his 2015 Christmas card?

Debbie got me a putting green in our backyard for my birthday to inspire me to get out and do something. Like her making me walk three miles a day wasn't enough?

Each day is getting a little better, and we have the surgery pain under control and heading in the right direction. I have about two or three more weeks of recovery and then I can lift more than a gallon of milk. Then maybe, just maybe, my dear daughters, Mandy and Jessica, will allow me to lift a Q-tip to clean my ears!

Thanks again so much for all the thoughts, prayers, and kind words; they are truly appreciated.

This is the numbness I mentioned earlier.

2 Down, 10 to Go!!!
November 18, 2014

Yesterday was our second chemo treatment of twelve. As I was sitting waiting for all the fun and poking to begin, I let my mind wander, people-watching and thinking of all kinds of things to pass the time away.

Today, while watching all the people coming in for treatment and picking where to sit, I got Billy Joel's "Piano Man" stuck in my head. *But of course,* I thought, *how well that fits this treatment center.* So I started to ad-lib the words (of course, to myself) and came up with the following couple of verses to amuse myself.

It's nine o'clock at BJC.
The regular crowd shuffles in.
There's an old man sitting next to me
Makin' jokes as his chemo pumps in.

He said, "Son, what chemo are you in here for?
Is it Vectibix, 5FU, or Irinotecan?
We're all in here for one or more,
And I hope it's no more than four!"

Now Jim and Carla are really good nurses;
They get me my chemo for free,
And they are good with a joke and access my port,
But there is someplace that I'd rather be.

It's a pretty good crowd for a Monday morning,
And Dr. Lim gives me smile

'Cause he knows he has given me a chance for a cure,
To forget about cancer for a while!

And my chemo pump sounds like a carnival,
Meaning the last drops have now passed through!
As soon as I'm unplugged from all the pumps,
Deb and I will be out of this place!

OK, so it won't reach the top 50, but I have to do something to amuse myself.

These past two weeks have been different from the last ten months of treatment. They seem harsher, but after being off chemo for seven weeks before and after surgery, maybe my chemo memory has forgot about the harsh times, so maybe they're not so bad after all?

I am typing this with two fingers—OK, so I always type with two fingers, but these are the only ones that do not have the chemo-causing finger splits, and luckily they are on opposite hands. Sometimes you have to look hard for luck!

And I don't want to talk about my sixteen-year-old acne face. I need a 5-gallon bucket of Clearasil!

Well, my two fingers are getting tired. Keep those kind notes, words, and prayers coming, and they are truly appreciated.

Deb and I wish y'all a Happy Thanksgiving! (I threw that "y'all" in there for our Atlanta family connection).

Thanksgiving Report
December 1, 2014

Thanksgiving is by far Deb's and my favorite holiday—no presents, just everyone's presence is required for food, drinks, and conversation. A long time ago we would go to my mom and dad's house around noon for the Dugo Thanksgiving Turkey Feast. After we were all stuffed, we head over to Deb's mom and dad's house at 4:00 for the Fear's Thanksgiving Turkey Feast and get double stuffed!

After several years and pounds later, Deb and I decided to have Thanksgiving at our house for both families and let our moms each cook and bring the turkey and dressing. Our moms jumped on that idea, and so began, thirty-eight years ago, the "whose turkey and dressing did you like the best?" competition! I kid you not; each mom would corner me and drill me with that question, and of course they were both the best!

Sadly, our parents are gone now, but the Thanksgiving tradition lives on, along with the turkey competition. I grill one turkey, and our son-in-law Dan smokes another turkey (damned if I know how he keeps it lit), and of course mine is always better. The dressing is another matter; we have not had dressing to match our moms' dressing yet, although my sister Barb's dressing is as close as you can get. Bottom line: we had a great Thanksgiving and we have so much to be thankful for—family, friends, and our health.

After writing "health," I thought, *I guess that sounds funny with my situation. However, all things considered in 5 months, 7 days, 12 hours and 14 seconds (but who's counting?) I should be declared cured!* So you see we are thankful for our present health and future health.

These past two weeks have been rather rough. We only had four good days out of fourteen, and thank God the good days started on Thanksgiving. They sent us out a $400 (my cost: $59) drug to get me feeling better the day before Thanksgiving, and it worked. I would have paid the $400 at that point. The pharmacist, Torrey (we are on a first-name basis), told me this drug is so old it's older than aspirin. The patent ran out and a new company makes it, charging this ungodly price, and calls it Opium Tincture. He opens the bottle to let me smell it, at which point I tell him it smells like the paregoric that my mom use to give me for everything, and he replies, "Yep that's it!" So now it's called opium. Hmm . . . that would explain a lot about some of the things I did in my youth.

We are just completing our third chemo, with nine to go, so we will be slipping and sliding our way home here shortly. Again, thanks for all your prayers, kind and witty comments, and support. Deb and I truly appreciate it all!

Christmas Wishes
December 15, 2014

Deb and I want to wish everyone a very Merry Christmas and a Happy and Safe New Year—2015! It is hard to believe it has been twelve months, as of December 27, since I was diagnosed with stage 4 cancer, with no cure and twenty-four months to live. Since then, we have been given a chance for a cure (and we took it), with surgery (and we did it), and six months of chemo (and we're doing it). And here we are, four months away from finding out if the surgery and chemo have cured the cancer and if we can start living life again, as opposed to just surviving!

It has been one hell of a ride, but the last two weeks have been good. I got back into doing some projects, BBQ, and walking two nine-hole rounds of golf, and I am feeling more and more normal.

Last March, we walked in the UNDY 500 in Forest Park, which raises money to fight colon cancer. I entered a team and everybody came back to our house for BBQ and drinks after the walk. Well, we are doing it again on March 28, 2015. Again I entered a team under a new team name: "No Colon and Still Rolling." (How is that for a team name? Thanks, Denise!) Should you want to join us, here is the website to sign up with our team for the "2015 St. Louis Undy Run/Walk." Click the "Join a Team" link and look for my name as captain, or look for the team name, and again, everyone is invited back to our house for BBQ and beverages after the walk/run. Deb and I will be doing the one-mile walk, not the run.

We have a busy week and a half of doctors' appointments before Christmas: chemo today, colon doctor Wednesday, liver doctor Friday, and CT scan on December 22. Does that sound like fun or what? However, we just completed our fourth chemo treatment with eight to go—sounds better each day.

Deb and I want to thank everyone for all the support, prayers, and kind words they have been giving us!

Double Dog Dare New Year's
December 24, 2014

Deb and I have always had a dog, sometimes two dogs. However, the two dogs were usually not by choice. On a couple of occasions, we were asked to keep a stray or rescue dog until they found a home for it. Little did I know we would end up providing a home for the stray dog. It has been about fifteen years since we have had two dogs, and everything in the universe seems to be just fine having one dog, till now.

Deb seems to think a second dog will cure my cancer and make us young again. Betty, our dog, and I are not so sure about this. On top of this, Deb wants a little lap dog of the type that I always associate with yappy dogs that bark at any and everything. Now thanks to her sister Denise, Deb's Facebook is blown up with all kinds of little yappy dogs that need a home, jumping around like Andy Taylor's deputy, Barney Fife (Don Knotts) on *The Andy Griffith Show*.

I reluctantly have agreed to entertain the idea of a second dog as long as it is not a yapper, that Betty likes it without eating it, that it cures my cancer, and that it doesn't look or act like Barney (nervous and waving an empty gun around).

We have visited several rescue websites, and, much to my luck, they are all hard to navigate, and you can't talk with anybody. We had to leave messages that cut us off before we were finished, write emails that would not go through due to an error, and fill out an online adoption application that would not let you type in any of the spaces—and get this: it was a three-page application that asked questions like, "How many playdates a week will you schedule? What is your monthly income?" and so on! It was more involved than adopting a child. Come on, it's a dog! It was like I designed their websites. SWEET! Actually, I think these so-called "rescue facilities" are dog hoarders and don't want to let go of any of their dogs. Just saying.

I had a CT scan this past Monday, and our oncology doctor called and told us some really good news: all the repaired spots on the liver have shrunk considerably and everything else looks really good, so the plan now is to continue with the chemo for another two months and then do an MRI that will show if there is any trace of cancer anywhere. I will still have another two months of chemo, even if the MRI shows no cancer, just to make sure there is no cancer hiding. Looking at the BIG picture, we can handle that.

So maybe there is something to Deb's logic and belief that a second dog will cure my cancer? Wow, I can just see the headlines: "Second dog cures cancer where chemo failed, Debra Dugo wins the Noble Peace Prize!" So Deb's search for a second dog will continue, while Betty and I wait with bated breath. I am trying to train Betty to be a 60-pound lap dog, but it's not going very well—she is rather big and it's painful when she tries to sit on my lap.

This news was a great Christmas present and a good way to start the 2015 New Year. It is Christmas Eve, and we are so looking forward to getting the family together tonight and having Santa visit the grandkids to kick this holiday season off to a big start.

Deb and I wish you all a Merry Christmas and a Safe and Happy New Year!

2015 Missions, 2 Down, 1 to Go!
January 5, 2015

Mission 1 was a second dog for Deb, and we did it. We went to an adoption event at a PetSmart Sunday and found Flo. She is a Chihuahua-terrier mix, but she looks more terrier and that's a good thing. She's supposed to be two years old, no tail (not sure what happened to the tail), one frost bit ear, apparently had a litter or two of puppies because she has rather large nipples for a two-year-old. There was a lot of barking going on from all the other strays, but none from Flo, which was the deal sealer. But, boy, is she a lover (that would explain the litters)! She took to Deb and Deb took to her, so we took her home. Reading through Flo's records, it said she was dumped at a man's house who called and said if the rescue center would not pick her up, he would shoot her. What kind of a moron would do that?

Flo and Betty are doing pretty good coexisting. Flo is kind of housebroken, but not totally. She has all her shots, a microchip, has been spayed (not soon enough), and has a cough, so off to our vet to have her checked out. The vet said all looks good except she has kennel cough.

Kennel cough, what the . . . ? Sounds like a breakfast cereal that would be on the shelf between Captain Crunch and Count Chocula. So now we have some antibiotics to give her, and we have to try to keep Betty away from her because it is contagious. Hmmmm . . . and *this* is the dog that will cure my cancer?

Mission 2: Buy an upright exercise bike for myself. I sent an email to my friends saying I was in the market for an exercise bike (also known as a clothes hanger). Well, my buddy Ed Regelean called and told me he started hanging some clothes up in his basement and found an exercise bike, "So come and get it, no charge!"

It's a really good DP Aerodyne bike, and after my first session with it, it kicked my butt in three minutes and less than a mile. This bike has handlebars that move back and forth as you ride, so you are getting an upper workout along with your lower workout. It also has this BIG fan in the front, hooked to the pedals, that gives the resistance as you pedal and blows air around to keep you cool. It is also very loud.

While I ride, I watch the golf channel and get all the latest instructions and tips that really screw up my game. However, I had to turn the volume up so loud that Deb came downstairs to see if I had a new chemo side effect and was going deaf. So off to the store to buy headphones for the TV, which cost more than a new bike. Can I catch a break, now that I have a little dog that is pooping in the house and I'm exercising with these BIG goofy ear thingies on?

Mission 3 is to be Cancer-free in 2015. Well, we got the dog that cures cancer, I put all my weight back on, I'm exercising and getting my strength back, and I have an

MRI in a couple of months to prove I'm Cancer-free. So you see, we are well on our way to a Super 2015, starting now and escalating at the end of April!

We had a really good New Year's Eve—our grandkids Truman and Remy spent the night with us. After fireworks at Westport, carryout from McDonald's, TV and video games, and everyone in bed at 9:30, what more could you ask for?

This would not have happened without all the encouragement and support you gave Deb and our family! It is truly a blessing to have family and friends like you. I thank all of you from the bottom of my heart for everything you have done for us these past twelve months!

Resolutions
January 12, 2015

Each year people ask me what my New Year's Resolutions are. I have never made any. It always seemed like I would think of some goofy adventure I would try, something like jumping out of an airplane, climbing a mountain, swimming with the sharks, etc. Not that those are goofy, they just weren't anything like I'd wanted to do in the following twelve months. So I always refrained from making a New Year's resolution. I usually had goals and a pretty good idea of what I wanted to accomplish in the upcoming year, and they did not always work out, so why put extra stress on myself, trying to do something out of the ordinary in a time frame?

The other day I was working on some drawings for a library table I'm making for Deb and needed our dictionary—yes, we still have one—to look up a word, as there's no spell check on my pencil, and I was in the R section and saw the word "resolution." It had a long definition, so out of curiosity, I read it. It said nothing about New Years! Actually, I was having a hard time figuring out where it linked up with New Year's resolutions, and toward the end, it's defined as "A formal statement of opinion or decision, agreed to after the consideration of a motion." Well, OK, I guess that is close enough.

However, what caught my attention and got me thinking is that it also stated the following, "The quality of not allowing difficulties or opposition to affect one's purpose!" Well, that got me thinking about resolutions in a different light, what with our situation we are facing this year.

So here is my very first New Year's resolution: I plan on beating cancer before the end of 2015! I will continue to exercise, and I started working back in my shop building a bedroom set for Deb. Being busy these past two weeks has really helped us stay positive and feel productive, and that, my friends, is a really, really good thing!

Don't get me wrong, we're not going into this blind. We still know there is a possibility I may still have some cancer after my MRI in April. So, keeping that in mind, we feel we won't be devastated if the results come back positive. However, our oncology doctor has a nonintrusive plan should it still show some cancer signs.

Either way, we are moving forward with an active, busy 2015. Jump out of an airplane, climb a mountain, swim with the sharks—nope, none of that, but we are planning golf, travel, and a Soap Box Derby with our grandson Truman; also, our grandkids' basketball games, baseball games, and swim meets are all in our plans. Oh yeah! The bedroom set for Deb! Got to work that in, too.

Well, it's time to leave for the BJC Country Club for cocktail hour. We have a late appointment today, and I hope they have some pretzels left when we get there. Thanks for all the thoughts, notes, and prayers.

Explaining Cancer to a 7- and 5-Year-Old
January 26, 2015

I started this journal entry two weeks ago and struggled with this subject. Deb and I have been day-caring for our daughter's babies, Truman and Remy, Monday through Friday. We have done this since they were born. However, being as they are both in school now, our hours have been cut to 7 a.m. till 8:45 a.m. when we drop them off for school. Then Deb and I are footloose and fancy free to sit around and stare at each other and wonder what we are going to do the rest of the day.

Truman and Remy are very observant and curious, so they knew something was different with me after the two hospital stays and my being missing in action during recovery. Plus, when I did get back in action, I laid around a lot and wanted to just read them books, not run around the house playing games.

They came to visit me in the hospital and at Siteman during one of my treatments and saw all the tubes and bags of chemo hooked up to me. They had a lot of questions about all the tubes and bags, but not about why I was in there, and that was OK with me at the time. But now, they are more curious about what was wrong and whether I am going to get better. I think it's because, in the games we play before school, I don't move as fast and have to rest at different times and suggest we read a book.

LEO DUGO

A couple of the games we play are Spy Mouse. I'm usually the mouse, trying to get the cheese they hide, and they are the cats, trying to get the mouse before I get the cheese. They are very fast, so I make them crawl on all fours to give me a chance, but they still get me. They are very fast crawlers. I'm slow and always the loser, whether I'm the mouse or the cat.

The other game is Angry Bird Star Wars. I am the PigBot on the Evil side; I take the place of Darth Vader. They are the Angry Birds that take the place of Luke Skywalker and Princess Leia. The only way I know this is because they tell me all the names and what they do and what planet they come from. I'm lost most of the time, and again I lose and they win. The good thing about this game is they shoot my space ship down, and I crash-land on the couch for repairs, and I stay there for long periods of time for major repairs!

Lately, they have been asking more direct questions about what was wrong with me and what is in my "Murse." I named my colostomy storage bag that has all my emergency supplies in it a Murse, because men don't carry a purse. If I ever get mugged and the muggers steal my Murse, they will be in for a big surprise and disappointment when they rifle through it looking for money and valuables; they will be left holding the bag—literally!

So I figured now was the time to educate them about cancer and the type and cause of my cancer—of course, after I talked to Jessica and Dan about how I would approach this subject. I thought long and hard about how to approach this without making them sad, but I realized I'm on the way to recovery. So I decided to explain cancer using our Angry Birds Star Wars as the theme, and it went like this:

"Cancer is like a bad Pigbot from the Dark Side, like the Star Wars we play. I got my bad Cancer Pigbot from breathing a fiber called asbestos, which they are not allowed to use anymore. However, one other way you can get it is from smoking cigarettes, so you don't ever want to do that! Anyway, the Cancer Pigbot was flying around in my body and landed in my colon." (I drew a stick man with a big body for illustration and organ location.) "They set up camp there in my colon—" Of all places to camp, and they picked the colon, I would have to fire that scout for picking the place next to a dump. "—and grew a very big camp with lots of Pigbots. So they decided to start exploring and set up more camps in my body. So first they went to my lymph nodes and set up a smaller camp, then off to my liver and set up several small camps, and then the last camp they set up was another small camp in my left lung.

"I went to my doctor for a checkup because I felt some-thing was not quite right, and that is when they saw the big Cancer Pigbot's camp in my colon. Then after an x-ray, just like when Truman broke his arm, they found all the other Cancer Pigbots. The doctor said, 'Here is the plan: we will operate and go in the colon and remove the giant Cancer Pigbots camp and capture all Cancer Pigbots in the camp and put them in prison. Then we will send in chemo Angry Bird Bots that will Laser Zap all the other Cancer Pigbot's that are hiding everywhere else in the body.' This will take some time to find and zap them all, but we should have them all and I will be Cancer Pigbot–free in twelve weeks, around the middle of April. And, at that time, I will be able to catch both of you in our Star Wars and Spy Mouse games. So enjoy your victories now, because I will be the King Pigbot and Ruler of Spy Mouse, the Grand Poo-Papa of all games!"

They said, "No way! You will still be OLD."

Talk about taking the wind out of my sails! Anyway, it went well, and the only question they had was what could they have for a snack, and I think they think Truman's broken arm was more serious, and that's a good thing at this point. And who knows? By the time they reach their teens, someone may find a cure, and cancer will be on the same level as a broken arm. OK, so that is some powerful wishful thinking, but they have made some great strides and cures in the past thirteen months.

So now my two typing fingers are weary and tired, and I'm putting them to bed, along with the rest of me.

Thanks again for all the thoughts, comments, and prayers! Deb and I enjoy and appreciate them all.

Better Days Ahead!
February 16, 2015

Two weeks ago, Sunday, February 8, Deb woke up with a pain in her stomach, thinking she had a touch of the stomach flu. However, it was such a beautiful day, sunny and mid-sixties, she wanted to walk 9 holes of golf and thought this would go away. Off we went and after 5 holes, she'd had enough and quit. She spent the rest of the day lying around and I became the nurse.

Monday wasn't any better, and she became achy, hot and then cold but no fever, still thinking it was the flu until the evening she started thinking it was something else. Tuesday, we saw the doctor, and after pushing around on her stomach, they sent us to the hospital (our country club) for a CT, thinking it may be her appendix. It was diverticulitis, and it was abscessed, meaning it caused a small hole in the colon, and they admitted her to the hospital for three days. They caught it early enough that they were able to heal it with three straight days of strong antibiotics and no food.

Thursday, they released her to come home, along with more antibiotics and a limited diet. The pain is gone and she is slowly getting her strength back, along returning to a normal diet. The good news is she is seeing my colon surgeon, Dr. Silvera. (Funny what we consider good news these days.) He said if you are over fifty, you have a good chance of getting this, and Deb stands a good chance of not getting it again. The old myth that eating nuts and popcorn caused this is not true. They really don't know what causes this. It just happens, and luckily we caught it early and did not need an operation.

We didn't see this coming, and we are finding more and more people who have gone through this. Who knew? Things are getting back to normal, whatever that is, and we are creeping up on spring and warmer weather.

About a month ago, I mentioned we are walking in the 2015 Undy Walk / Run, March 28 at Forest Park, and then coming back to our house for BBQ and beverages. So far we have seven people on our team. Should you want to join us, go to www.undyrunwalk.org, click on "St. Louis," and enter our team name, "No Colon and Still Rolling," or my name as the captain. If they ask for a password, you will have to enter your own password. Hope to see you there!

Random Thoughts and a New Normal
February 23, 2015

First, a Debbie report: She is doing great! The pain is gone, the tenderness is gone, and she has her strength back. She only has a few more days of the medication, and we can toast to a quick recovery.

Just completing my ninth of twelve chemo treatments, and my mind is running wild, so I'll share some of these thoughts with you (of course, not all of them). I think back to last August 2014, when our doctor gave us a chance to cure my cancer and explained the surgery would not be easy, nor had this procedure been tried on anyone with stage 4 cancer. However, it gave us a chance to live a normal life. I was not worried about the surgery. The part that bothered me the most was living with a colostomy bag (I'll refer to it as "CB") and trying to figure out how that could be normal.

We are going on six months since the surgery and about six weeks from finishing our chemo treatments, and I'm still trying to figure out how this "normal" thing is going to work. I know after the chemo stops, things will get better—no more neuropathy in my hands and feet, no more split fingers and toes, no more rashes, no more fatigue, no more split lips, no more confusion and chemo brain (I hope, or at least less), no more mouth sores, and other things I won't mention. So you see, this will get better, much better, but I still have to deal with the CB!

Trust me, I have tried to make friends with it for the past five months, and every time I start to build some confidence that we are friends, it turns on me when I'm not expecting it and shatters our friendship. And who knows? After the chemo stops, maybe it will start liking me and we can learn to live together, and if that happens, I can get back to living a more normal life, although it will be a new normal.

I sat down the other day and started to think of all the things that would fall into the new "normal" category:

- Limited sleeping positions (I have three)

- Limited clothes options (I can't tuck a shirt in, but can wear big pants and suspenders—kind of goofy-looking, but it goes with my hairstyle at the moment)

- Always traveling or leaving the house with the Murse (forgetting it kind of ruins the moment or event)

- Showering

- Driving (I drive with a Tupperware divided sandwich container that keeps the seatbelt from crushing the CB)

- Bending over to tie my shoes or pick the golf ball out of the cup (maybe I'll get more gimmes, of course not from Deb—she cuts me NO slack)

I'm sure there will be more as time goes on. Don't get me wrong. I'm not regretting that I chose this route because it gave us a chance to beat stage 4 cancer. Also I'm not complaining. Like I said, these are random thoughts. It's just a different lifestyle, and I am trying to figure out how to make the best of the situation and go on living a happy and productive life.

It has made me realize how many simple things we do every day that I took for granted. And who knows? With time, these too might become simple, and my new normal will be my normal without a second thought.

Then I got to thinking about my dad. As a kid, he lost his left foot in a train accident. All he had was the heel of his left foot, and he lived with an artificial foot, but you would never know it except for a slight limp when he walked. He was a pilot, and flew in the Civil Air Patrol in World War II. He flew and sold airplanes all over the United States, and I never heard him complain about his foot. He had a new normal and adjusted to it.

Then I think about all the children I have seen with cancer, missing limbs, and life-threatening diseases, and I realize that I'm pretty lucky to have gone seventy years without having to deal with something like this. Yes, I have had my share of broken bones, but those heal and you move on, so that's where I'm at now, trying to figure out this new normal and move on.

I just had my first experience with rejection because I think they think I have cancer cooties—and this was from an adult we knew.* Deb didn't think that was the case when I told her what happened, but I really believe that was the case. It was awkward and uncomfortable, but with my present rash and acne from the chemo, I can see how an uninformed person could think that. Then I thought how hard it could be on a child with cancer, experiencing that kind of rejection. So the point of this is, please educate your children and grandchildren that cancer is not contagious.

Well, this has been a long post, and I think I'm about thought out for the day. Deb and I thank everyone for your thoughts, prayers, and kind words—they are pick-me-uppers!

---

*Here's what happened: Deb was asked to substitute on our old bowling league, so I went along and brought my bowling ball in case they need another sub, which they did. However, they chose to bowl shorthanded rather than allow me to join them.

Trending UP!
March 9, 2015

Our daughter Jessica used the term *trending up* when I was in the hospital recovering after the surgery in September, so I thought it would be appropriate to use it again at this point. Last Friday, I had a CT and meetings with our oncology and liver doctors to see if I was cancer-free, and I'm not. They were very excited to tell me the only cancer I have left is in the liver, and all the cancer spots are shrinking at an aggressive rate. Although we were hoping for a cancer-free report and it was not what we wanted to hear, it is still good news. However, we were prepared that I still had cancer.

I was expecting a negative report because I believe my liver infusion pump quit working four weeks ago, but I didn't know for sure. Four weeks ago, they installed 30 cc of heparin, after two weeks they normally drain 10 cc of heparin out and then install 30 cc of chemo. Two weeks ago, they drained 29 cc of heparin out, meaning the pump was not pumping. My concern was whether I would get these next two weeks of chemo. Plus, my rash and acne were getting better, which meant the chemo was not working— that's a necessary evil, for the rash and acne to be going strong. Then, all of a sudden, six days ago, the rash and acne started to come back with a vengeance. Woo-hoo!

We had several discussions with all the doctors about the pump situation, and they told me sometimes that happens and then it starts again, so we are hoping that's what happened, and we will know shortly when they drain the pump. We also have a backup plan, in which they will remove the pump if it isn't working and administer the liver chemo through my power port in my chest (the Door Bell) because they can't replace the pump. We can send a man to the moon but we can't replace my belly pump? What the...?

I am currently getting my tenth chemo treatment with two to go, then another CT and maybe an MRI, which will show better cancer images. But we can't do an MRI with the pump in, and who knows? By then, perhaps I'll be cancer-free. However, this has not been free—over $60K out of pocket and still counting.

Our question to both doctors was, if I'm not cancer-free after my last treatment and the chemo is not shrinking the tumors anymore, then what? They have more tricks up their sleeve and explained some of our options,* which I'm sure I won't need them because I plan to be cancer-free!

Here is what I just now found out: Bad news, Good news. Bad news is, the pump doesn't work. Good news is, the pump doesn't work, and they will probably remove it. So now we wait for the backup plan. If they can't jump start the pump again, where do we go from here?

---

*This included lung surgery and an immune therapy trial if I were to qualify.

Well, I'm toast and done for the day, I'm sure this will all work out. Just got to keep thinking, *ten treatments down and two to go!*

See ya.

To Pump or Not to Pump?
March 23, 2015

That was the question last week, so they set us up for some additional pump testing last Thursday. The test showed the dye they inserted in the pump did transfer to the liver, but they were not sure why it was not transferring the chemo, nor if I would get the correct dose of chemo through the pump.

So now the plan for this morning was to drain the pump and see how much chemo is left in it, with two contingent plans. Well, lo and behold, the pump started working again. It must have got word I was already planning to have it removed and got scared of losing its warm little hideaway.

We are now back on track with one more treatment in fourteen days. I say that, but our doctor wants to put me on a chemo maintenance program after my next CT scan consisting of chemo pills and/or one chemo treatment in my port every three weeks. The result of the CT will determine the treatment. I can hardly wait!

Last week was a really good week for us. We felt good, played golf (we won't talk about score), had BBQ, and sat out on the porch, just like old times. However, the week before was the week from HELL! And that was as much my fault as anybody's. That Monday was chemo day, and that leaves me feeling a little punk for a couple of days with some real unpleasant side effects. A while back, the doctors said I needed to get the basal cell skin cancer removed from the bridge of my nose, so what the hell was I thinking when I had it scheduled for the day after chemo? Actually, I didn't think it would be a big deal because it was outpatient, and they would just zap it and I would be out of there—NOT. Six hours, three skin scrapings to the bone, and twenty-three stitches (I do have a rather large nose—thanks, Dad!) later, we were out of there! If that wasn't enough, between skin scrapings, I used the bathroom and dropped my glasses in the toilet, and of course it was right before I flushed. Really, can I catch a break?!

They gave me pain pills, and my nose had a bandage that looked like the front bumper off an 18-wheeler truck. I thought, *What are the pain pills for? I have no pain at all!* And then the stuff they used to numb my nose wore off—give me the damn pain pills! So I was in la-la land Tuesday night and Wednesday, and the pain meds were not playing well with my chemo meds. Then came Thursday—infusion pump testing—and that was also real pleasant. I'll leave it at that. Friday got better, and I was recovered for the weekend.

We are really excited about spring and warmer weather. As I mentioned about three or four weeks ago, Deb and I are kicking off this spring by walking in the Colon Cancer UNDY 5000 this Saturday, March 28, at Forest Park. Our team name is "No Colon and Still Rolling," and I'm pleased to say we have eighteen team members.

After the walk, everybody is coming back to our house for BBQ, drinks, and conversation. If the weather is good, we will plan a putting contest on the putting green.* Deb got me for my seventieth birthday, so bring your putter, or use one of ours. Don't worry about balls—we got plenty of them.

All the chemo pumps just went off, signaling I'm done, so we are out of here. Thanks for all your support, thoughts, prayers, and comments. They are truly appreciated.

---

*I found out that when I played golf or built a piece of furniture in my shop, it completely occupied my mind. I forgot about cancer, and it made things seem more normal and gave me a feeling of accomplishment. I would look forward to it, and it helped with my mental state and attitude. If you have a hobby or are passionate about something, get busy and jump in with both feet. You will be surprised how much better you feel.

12th of 12 Treatments & Pump Kaput!
April 6, 2015

The title of this post kind of says it all. Today was the last scheduled chemo treatment. We are hoping the CT in two weeks will show that I'm cancer-free. The liver pump issue we have been dealing with once again did not give me the correct dose of 5FU chemo, so they are sending me home today with the fanny pack pump to wear for the next three days. Luckily, it is black so I have shoes and a belt to match—I hate it when my outfits don't match.

They are infusing some special magic solution into the pump to see if it starts the pump again. I agreed, thinking it may help someone else down the road, being as this is the first time this has happened to these pumps. But bottom line, I'm having this one removed in the next two weeks, and if they can't replace it, that's OK with me. So in a couple of weeks, we will know the status of the cancer and what chemo maintenance program they will put me on. Thinking positive thoughts!!!

Whoops, just found out the special magic solution didn't work. This was funny. I guess Deb and I were worn out from all the Easter excitement yesterday. At Siteman Cancer Center, they have one room in each pod that has a bed, which they use to access my liver pump, as I have to lie flat for the procedure. So they finished, and I was getting the two other chemo drugs in my port but starting to doze, and so was Deb. I jokingly invited Deb to hop in bed with me for a snooze, and she did, and it's just a small twin bed!

I think they are renaming the room "The Honeymoon Suite."

Easter was great. We had the whole family over, Tom and Denise brought an awesome ham, and everyone brought a yummy side dish. The weather was perfect, so we were able to have an egg hunt outside for Truman and Remy. We also used the putting green and learned we all need a lot of putting and chipping practice.

Deb and I wish everyone a belated Happy Easter and good health!

Not Done Yet & Mindset
April 17, 2015

With all that has happened in the last sixteen months, I got to thinking about all the different mindsets we have experienced, from doom and gloom, negative to positive, and everything in between. To say the least, it has been a real challenge, learning experience, and roller-coaster ride (without a seat belt) for Deb and me. But things are looking up and the future looks brighter—not to say there won't be some bumps in the road, and there will be in our senior years, but that is to be expected. I guess you could say that's a mindset right there!

The mind is a funny thing and can take us on so many adventures, good and bad. The trick seems to be understanding the bad and figuring out how to overpower it, dissect it, and turn it in to a positive, and that's not always easy. I'll describe each of these different mindsets as a "bad thing" or a "good thing."

Thinking back to December 2013 when they told us if we did radiation and chemo I would have about twenty-four months to live—bad thing. My thought process was to get everything in order, and I mean everything! All the projects that were on the back burner got moved to the front burner, and that was a good thing.

All of those projects that I would have done myself I

could not physically do because of the treatments and side effects—a bad thing. I contracted out some new windows, doors, and garage doors to be installed and oversaw the installation—a good thing. I felt like the boss, although I knew Deb was.

Thinking about not seeing our daughters and grand-children grow up was a bad thing, but we kept active with them and cherished every moment, which was a good thing.

Then came August 2014, a chance for a cure, a really good thing! Although they explained there was no guarantee for the cure and the operation would be rough, it was the best and only chance I had to survive. Another good thing.

The operation was rough and the recovery was not much better. I was thinking, *What the hell have I done?* A bad thing. Living with a colostomy bag has presented a new lifestyle for us—a bad thing, but getting better. I realize now how many simple, everyday things I did and took for granted. It made me look back at the last seventy years and appreciate them even more and that's a good thing, kind of.

Now that we are seven months past the operation and each CT keeps looking better, I could be cancer-free this year, which is a really good thing. Thinking about living a longer life—cancer-free, that is—got me thinking about how much longer we might be talking about.

Not to sound ungrateful for this second chance, but sometime in the last couple of weeks, the news showed the oldest person alive, a 116-year-old woman, and she didn't look like she knew she was alive! God bless her, she died the next day, and another, 115-year-old women took her place as the oldest person alive, and she, too, died the next day! I don't want to be in that category, and I don't think I have to worry about it. You see, I'm not afraid to die; I'm just not ready yet. There are still things I want to do, but I need to be healthy and in a good mindset to enjoy what lies ahead for us, and I believe we are on the right track in both areas.

That being said, we just had our CT today and met with our oncology doctor. We did not get as good a piece of news as we anticipated. However, I'm not surprised because of the pump issues. My blood test when I was diagnosed in 2013 showed my tumor markers were 6, and anything below 3 is normal, so the Cancer Pigbots (to borrow from the description I used for the grandkids) were having a party inside me.

After the surgery, my tumor markers went down to 1.6. Their party was over, at least we thought. The last couple months they started to rise, and today they are 3.7. The CT showed everything is continuing to shrink, but being as I missed two treatments because of the pump malfunction, we are staying on the chemo schedule for two more months and hitting them a little harder to make up for lost time and missed chemo. This is really OK. Yes, my markers have risen, but they are real close to being below 3, so in these next two months we should be in good shape for the maintenance program. And they believe they have a fix for the pump, and if so, that's really good news, because the pump delivers the chemo directly to the liver where all the Cancer Pigbots are trying to get the party started again.

So here we are back to another mindset, and it's a good one because we are moving in the right direction. Deb and I are feeling good, back to playing golf, and looking forward to watching Truman and Remy playing on their ball and swim teams this summer. And Truman will be racing in the All-American Soap Box Derby in St. Louis in June. We just started building the car, and watching him building the car and turning the wrenches puts a smile on my face from ear to ear!

These good mindsets would not be possible without the support we get from our family and friends. Your thoughts, prayers, and comments mean more than words can say! When I need a pick-me-up, I will go back to all your comments everyone has posted on our Caring Bridge Journals to help me stay positive.* As Elvis said, "Thank youuu! Thank you very much."

---

*As I mentioned before, after every journal entry I posted, our family and friends would post comments of encouragement. You can also get this type of support by attending support groups for whatever your situation is. Don't be shy—reach out. There are people who will help you.

Getting Pumped UP!
May 15, 2015

And believe you me, we are PUMPED UP! And here is why: the proposed pump fix WORKED! Everything is working and my liver is getting a direct and maximum chemo dose! Take that Cancer Pigbots!!!

The doctors and nurses are really happy to now have a fix when they have another pump problem, and so are we. And now for the rest of the story: We just got back from our oncology doctor visit, and he eliminated two of the chemo drugs and I will only get the 5FU chemo in the liver infusion pump this Monday! Then, June 2nd, I will get an MRI and PET scan, see Dr. Lim on June 5th, and if the scan looks good, we will do two more months of 5FU chemo treatments. Another scan after the two months of chemo, and if they look good, they will stop chemo treatment and do a scan every three months to make sure nothing is growing and NO MORE CHEMO!

They are having a hard time saying I will be cancer-free for fear it may return. I guess they have done this before and it came back. But I'm not afraid to say it when we reach that point in July, so I will be practicing it the next few weeks.

Deb and I are gearing up for a really busy month of June and looking forward to a good summer with lots of activities and spending time with our family and friends doing fun summer stuff.

I bought a new gas-powered hedge trimmer. Just what I needed. What was I thinking? It kicked my butt in twenty minutes, along with some poison ivy, and I had to rest the whole afternoon. I hid it in the toolshed, and, with chemo brain, I hope I can't find it again.

With this last scheduled chemo fast approaching, I got to thinking: I won't have much to report on this Caring Bridge site, and that's a good thing because I'm running out of things to say.

I have learned several things throughout this journey, but one of the most important things I knew before all this happened that has been reconfirmed and has reassured me is how important family and friends are and how not to take any of them for granted. We are all so different and unique in our own ways, and that's what makes us so special. I want to thank each and every one of you for the friendship and support you have given Deb and me!

The BIG Countdown!
June 5, 2015

Had an MRI and PET scan this past Tuesday, I called it my day in the TUBE! Just met with our oncology doctor and got the results . . . NO CANCER showed up on both scans! WOO-HOO!

So the plan now is two more months of chemo starting June 29 (I am getting a chemo break for the next three weeks). After the two months of chemo, we do another MRI and PET scan, if the scans are all clear again, NO MORE CHEMO and schedule scans for the next year to make sure nothing pops up.

As you can imagine, Deb and I are ecstatic, thrilled, jubilated, excited—oh yeah, and HAPPY!

June was going to be a big month for us, starting with our seven-year-old grandson, Truman, racing in the St. Louis All-American Soap Box Derby June 14th. It has been so much fun watching him put every bolt, washer, and nut together to build the car. Can't wait for June 14th—just watching him learn how to use the tools has been very rewarding.

Then June 25th kicks off a three-day golf tournament with our good friend Bob Sido. Bob, who I've mentioned before, is ninety-three, and I have a hard time keeping up with him, and that was before cancer! He is like Superman, without the tights and a cape, a true inspiration to me on how to age gracefully. We have played in this tournament for the past eight years or so, and we've never won, but we've come real close to winning. But with this news, who knows? This could be the year. If not, I feel like we won anyway by just being able to compete, have fun, and be cancer-free.

So starting June 29th, we start the BIG countdown till the end of August and NO MORE CHEMO! You cannot believe how good that sounds to us! Deb and I are so pumped. However, I don't think all of this has actually set in yet. I think our doctor was as surprised as we were. He said he never had a patient go from where I was eighteen months ago to being cancer-free, and I was in new territory in the cancer game.

All I can say at this point is, WOW and THANK ALL OF YOU for all your support through this journey!

Latest Update: I'm DONE!
June 5, 2015

When our team of doctors got the test results, our liver surgeon contacted the oncology doctor who developed the liver infusion pump in New York and sent her all my test results. He called us and wanted to meet with us today at 12:30 pm.

Well, after the team talked, they decided to end all chemo starting today because the scans showed no cancer, and they feared that if we continue with the chemo without cancer, I could become toxic.* We will keep the pump in and fill it with a special solution that will last four weeks to keep the pump from freezing up, do new MRI and PET scans in two months, and go from there.

So the countdown is over. That was the shortest two-month countdown I ever did!

I don't think I will post anything till we do the next set of scans—that is unless, Truman blows the field away . . . or Bob and I work a miracle at the golf tournament . . . but who knows? Some may consider this a miracle. Deb and I do! We are going to go have some fun and you should too.

---

*Meaning too much chemo and no cancer, which would leave me with extreme side effects and fatigued.

New Lease on Life!
June 28, 2015

OK, I know I said I was thinking about not writing for the next couple of months, but my mind is running wild with not having cancer and all the things I thought I would miss, and now realize I could be around for a lot more than I expected. So here it goes:

- All the prep, as far as getting things in order, was not in vain. It is a gift to Deb and the girls and has left me with a feeling of not having to worry about it, a relief of stress, and that's good.

- I hear or read all the testimonies about how having cancer has been a blessing, the sky is a brighter blue, the grass is greener, etc., etc. I never experienced that—not that I was walking around with my head down and thinking, *Poor me.* I just never experienced that it made everything brighter—it didn't. Just being honest. I was still thinking I had a good chance to kick cancer's ass if I kept a good attitude, did what my doctors said, exercised and ate right, but who knows what works?

- Getting to see our two daughters grow into adults—not that they aren't now, but seeing them enter their midlife phases will be fun, rewarding . . . and paybacks are hell. I'm so proud of both of them. They are so different and so much fun. Since my cancer diagnosis, we have had dinner at our house every Wednesday with Mandy and Jessica like it was going to be my last dinner, but

I fooled them. Those Wednesday dinners have been so much fun, uplifting, and made Deb and me laugh so much we talk about it until the next Wednesday. I love those girls so much. I knew that before all this happened, but I guess I could say it has made this aspect of my relationship with our daughters brighter and more fulfilling. Thank you, cancer!

- Getting to watch my two older grandsons figure out what floats their boats and move to the next phase of their lives will be real interesting and hopefully rewarding. I love them more than they know, and maybe I need to let them know.

- Getting to watch our younger grandchildren, Truman and Remy, graduate to first grade and second grade was a special gift, along with watching Remy's dance recital (best little Eskimo dancer ever). Their baseball games and swim meets have been so much fun! OK, they are still learning the basics, but getting to see what you didn't think you would get to see makes it better and more endearing.

- Friends. I knew Deb and I had good friends, but I didn't realize how good and how many friends we had until this journey began. They have been there for whatever we needed or thought we needed. They have helped keep our hopes up and willed us on to beat this, and we did!

Now let me tell you about Truman "Haybale" Brawner racing in the All-American Soapbox Derby on June 14th in St. Louis.

IT WAS A BLAST!!!

Don't get this race confused with the Pinewood Derby. He gets in the car and drives it down the hill. No engine, just gravity downhill racing. The car and driver can't weigh more than 200 pounds, so we had to add 80 pounds of weight to reach the 200 pounds max. This helps him go fast, but now we realize it makes it harder for him to stop after the finish line, especially if the pavement is wet, and it was. It rained eight times in a twelve-hour period.

The object is to drive in a straight line down the middle of his lane without swerving. Sounds easy, but watch people on the highway try to stay in their lane and you'll realize it's not that easy.

His first three races scared his mom, dad, Deb, and me, as he wove from the centerline to the hay bales protecting the curb, but never hit anything until after the finish line. They have a wall of hay bales way past the finish line to help stop any cars that get that far, and he crashed into the hay bales five times because he couldn't get the car completely stopped (thus the name "Haybale" Brawner). The really amazing thing was that he kept winning and kept driving straighter with each race. However, the hay bales took their toll on the front axle and spindles. He went all the way to the semifinals and took third place in the stock division, winning a trophy, toolbox, boomerang (it's on the roof), and some crazy hand-eye coordination game he and Remy love.

ATTITUDE DETERMINES ALTITUDE

All in all, it was a very fun day, and Remy is chomping at the bit to race with Truman next year as the "Double Trouble Racing Team! Featuring Truman 'Haybale' and Remy 'The Wild One' Brawner!"

Now for the rest of the story: We just finished up playing in the Glen Echo Member Guest golf tournament this weekend—18 holes Thursday, 27 holes Friday, and 18 holes Saturday. In a nutshell, we won our flight and went into a 5-hole shoot-out with 9 other teams to determine the overall winner and champions of the tournament. All though Bob and I were losing oil and smoking at the end of the day, we lasted three of the five shoot-out holes and came in 5th place overall—not bad for the team with the combined oldest age of 164 years! For winning our flight, we got a large crystal cup that will probably be Deb's new happy hour wineglass.

Well, it's 2:30 a.m., and I can't sleep because of these damn muscle cramps in my legs because of all this activity, but damn, it was worth it. So I'll walk around a little bit and go back to bed. Till next time, stay active, be happy and enjoy life, family, and friends!

Unchartered Territory
July 16, 2015

We met with our oncology doctor last Friday, and these are the words he used: "We are in unchartered territory!" He just got back from the Oncology Research Conference in Chicago. That's the same one he went to 2014 and came back and offered us a chance for a cure and we took it.

So now that we did the operation in 2014, and followed up with major chemo and now cancer-free, apparently they looked at each other and said now what? He is cancer-free at this moment, but what if there is some cancer not showing up on the scans, lying dormant and waiting for things to settle down and then start partying again. Thus the term "unchartered territory."

So here is the new plan: August 3rd MRI and CT. If it shows any cancer, we go full-blown chemo again—UGH! If no sign of cancer (like our last scan), we start a maintenance chemo program ("Baby Chemo," they called it) for the next eight months with another MRI/CT scans every two months, and depending on each scan, they will decide on the chemo treatment, Baby Chemo or Full-Blown Chemo. After eight months of scans and maintenance chemo and no signs of cancer, they are willing to deem me as "CANCER-FREE!" Meaning no more treatments, but I'm guessing they will want me to have some scans done periodically just to make sure nothing was missed. They said this Baby Chemo I could do standing on my head after what they pumped in to me the last eighteen months, so we will see. I started practicing standing on my head, and that's not so easy at this point.

It has been a really good summer of doing lots of fun summer stuff. We took a road trip to Arkansas to visit Deb's aunt and check on the Fear's Family Farm. At the farm, we stood around and kicked dirt clots and watched the beans and rice grow—pretty exciting stuff, kind of like watching paint dry!

Deb and our daughter Jessica upgraded their phones and insisted I upgrade my flip phone to one of their old smartphones. Reluctantly I agreed. All I wanted was a "PHONE to make calls on," but no, this one texts, tweets, takes photos, plays movies, washes clothes, and cooks dinner—what more could you want?

After one week with the smartphone, I got a message from AT&T that I had exceeded my International $100 call limit! What the hell are they talking about? I wondered. So I figured I'd been scammed. Jessica contacted AT&T and found out that I'd somehow returned a call I missed while trying to get the damn phone out of my pocket, and it was to Nigeria. No wonder I couldn't understand what they were saying! Anyway, I no longer have international service. They took it away from me, and that's just fine with me. I'm thinking another couple of weeks with the smartphone, and they will give me back my flip phone. You have to be smarter than the phone you have.

So till next time, keep your chin up and enjoy the rest of the year.

Good & Some Not-So-Good News!
August 8, 2015

Throughout this journey, I took the approach of being prepared for the worst and hoping for the best, and it has helped us move forward in a positive way. Last Monday I had a scan done, knowing it would show no signs of cancer again. We met with our oncology doctor yesterday for the results, and the really good news is there is no sign of cancer in my liver; however, there is a small 3mm spot in my left lung that has grown to 5mm. It is too risky for a biopsy or surgery because it is up against my aorta so the new plan is full-blown chemo, but a different method I have not experienced. I will get the standard liquid chemo in my port every three weeks and take six chemo pills every day Monday through Friday and get each weekend off to recover. We will do this for two months and have another scan to see if it did the job. However, he said if it becomes too tough on my system, I can reduce the dose or just do four days on the pills and three-day recovery.

This kind of set me back, but I now realize this may be the new normal for us, considering it originally spread throughout my body and now they start coming out when I'm off chemo any length of time. I have been off chemo for six weeks and have felt sooooo good, getting my strength back, slits on fingers and feet healed up, and acne gone—man, I thought we kicked cancer's butt, but not so much at this point.

This too shall pass, and I will be off chemo again in a couple of months and continue scans every two months, and we will make decisions on how to deal with whatever they throw at us. The summer is coming to a close, and it has been a really good one. I look forward to a good fall and winter.

On a lighter note, our granddaughter Remy and grandson Truman have a list of new words they learn every week. They learn to spell them, the definition, and how to use them in a sentence. One of Truman's words this week was "ancient" so Truman wrote the following sentence, "My papa is ancient!" (That's me.) What the—? I guess it's true. I can't catch either one of them anymore when we play tag or Spy Mouse!

Thanks for everyone's support, thoughts, prayers and comments. They help Deb and me get through all we have on our plate.

Nearing Expiration Date!
September 19, 2015

Ha! Back in December 2013, they gave me about twenty-four months and the last six months would be a downhill slide. Well we have about three months left, and I'm still going strong with no intention of slowing down! Nothing new has happened since my last post, so here is the latest scoop:

We are into our fifth week with three more weeks of this new chemo cocktail to go before our scan. It has been interesting to say the least. The first week was a cakewalk, only taking the six chemo pills a day. I thought, *No problem, this is like taking vitamins!* Second week, they infused the second chemo to join the pills . . . Whoa! Game on—all side effects came back in full force. However, no nausea, which is a real plus.

We met with our oncology doctor a week ago to see where we go from here and here it is:

Best-case scenario. If the scan in three weeks shows the spot in the lung is gone, or shrunk, we stay on the current chemo for two more months. Then another scan, and if it's gone completely, we take a short chemo break and start chemo maintenance program until all the future scans show I'm cancer-free.

Worst-case scenario. If the scan in three weeks shows the chemo has no effect on the spot, they want to do surgery and remove the spot.

The lung surgeon will have to be a REALLY GOOD salesman to convince me to have surgery again. I will go into the meeting with an open mind, but my torso has only about eight inches that have not been opened up front and back, and I'm not too keen to let them slice and dice the rest of me. Too bad they could not have closed me up with Velcro a year ago!

So there you go. Now you know as much as we do. Till the next scan, we will keep bumping along and making the best of things. Deb and I are looking forward to the fall, weather changes, holidays, and all the celebrations with family and friends. Thanks again for all the love and support everyone has given us. It is greatly appreciated!

One Scan Down, One to GO!
October 16, 2015

Finished the chemo treatment last week, had our scan this past Wednesday, and just met with our oncology doctor today hoping for a good report. As rough as these last eight weeks have been, I had to believe the chemo was doing some major cancer butt kicking! And it did!

The spot on my lung that had grown to 5mm has now shrunk to 2mm. They now know it was cancer but are not sure if the 2mm spot is cancer or just leftover scar tissue from the butt kicking. The only way to make sure is surgery, which our doctor and we are not in favor of, so the other way is eight more weeks of a reduced chemo treatment and if the scan shows no more growth, and it is still 2mm, it's scar tissue, WOO-HOO!!! If the spot is gone, that's even more awesome, A DOUBLE WOO-HOO, WOO-HOO!

Like I said, this will be a reduced chemo, no daily chemo pills. I will get Vectibix infusion every two weeks starting this Monday, October 19th, and our next scan mid December. Think about this, December 2013 is when they gave us the bad news. Now two years later, we get a second clean scan, and we beat cancer. Wow, what a great Christmas present that would be!

We are really excited at this point, and this good news gives us a lot to be thankful for. How fitting with our favorite holiday coming up: Thanksgiving! Deb and I love Thanksgiving—no presents, just family and friends getting together for dinner, drinks, and conversation and a chance to catch up on what's new and exciting in everybody's life's. One of our "Debbie Thanksgiving Traditions" is during dinner everybody has to state what they are thankful for. This produces a lot of eye rolls from our younger generation. We know and they think they know it all, but who knows, they may actually learn something from the "ancient" generation.

Deb and I wish everyone a Spooky Halloween and a Happy Thanksgiving!

Not Done Yet!
December 18, 2015

Had our second scan this past Tuesday and just met with our oncology doctor today. As much as we felt we would be cancer-free, it is not to be. The spot on my left lung that shrunk two months ago apparently has become immune to the chemo and is growing again. The new plan now is to have surgery and have it cut out—not the whole lung, just what they call a *wedge*. We meet with the lung surgeon on December 22 to discuss the surgery, recovery, and any other options. A couple of options we talked about was continue with stronger chemo, which I'm about chemo'ed out, or a round of radiation, which has some risk because the cancer is right up next to my aorta. Besides my last bout with radiation was not pleasant and put me in the hospital for over a week.* So the surgery looks like the best option at this point.

Now for some good news: they told me long ago that if anything was going to get me, beside Deb, it would be my daughters! Not really. It would be the cancer in my liver and the last four scans show NO CANCER, and that is really good news. Plus, the lung is the only place that this one little booger is showing off. He better enjoy this Christmas because it will be his last one!

This was when Jessica took over CaringBridge Journal entries for me.

The crazy thing is I'm feeling OK. If I could take away the chemo side effects, I think I would feel great. I have put weight back on and then some, but that is good because I will probably lose some after the surgery. That is one hell of a diet I would not recommend. I worry that my insurance company is going to put a HIT out on me when they find out more surgery bills are coming their way. However, they will be happy, as I will be, to see no more chemo after the surgery. Once we know more about the surgery and dates I'll post an update.

Deb and I wish everyone a very Merry Christmas, a Happy and Safe New Year's, and good health!

Decision Time
December 29, 2015

We met with our lung surgeon last week, and we really liked him. He answered all our questions and concerns. He explained the procedure and agreed to coordinate with our liver surgeon to remove the infusion liver pump at the same time (like a Happy Hour Surgery Special, 2 for 1). He also said, worst case, I would stay only one night at the hospital or maybe go home that day. Recovery will be four to six weeks, which were good selling points.

We are having the surgery to remove the spot on January 20, 2016 (the day after our forty-third wedding anniversary), which will allow me to be cancer-free. However, our doctors are telling us that because the colon cancer spread so much, some silent cells will probably pop up somewhere down the road, and we would start chemo again or more surgery. This is not what I wanted to hear, but it is what it is. Besides, surgery is now looking better than chemo. Get it cut out, four to eight weeks of recovery, and get on with your life, as opposed to ten to twelve months of chemo—*hmmm,* no brainer for me at this point.

What our doctor didn't see coming is that I am choosing not to undergo future chemo treatments (although Deb feels this is negotiable) should any of those stinking silent cancer cells show up down the road. I knew this time would come eventually, but I never knew when. The decision would be to continue on with the chemo treatment or stop the treatment. Notice, I did not say "quit" the treatment. The only thing I ever quit in my life was a job to go to a better one. And driving a race car, but I only quit that because it became a hazard to my marriage, family, and health. Priorities, it's all about priorities!

It isn't about how long I live. I feel it should come down to the quality of life I'm living and the good days outnumber the bad days. I have gone through several different chemo treatments and surgeries trying to beat cancer, and it has been quite a ride up to this point, but the bad days are outnumbering the good days and that's not good. Let me qualify that my bad days are from the chemotherapy sessions, not from any cancer symptoms or pain. The last two sessions have been getting me down physical and mentally, and that has taken a toll on me. I just think my system has a full tank of chemo, and my body is trying to tell me enough is enough.

When my dad retired, his answering machine message was "Hi, this is Skip Dugo, leave a message, hopefully I'm out doing something constructive!" That's pretty much how I feel. I want to be doing something constructive—not just existing on chemo and pain pills just to stay alive.

While I have been on chemo, I have not felt my best, but I pushed myself to do stuff so I would be constructive and live as close to a normal life as possible. During my chemo breaks, everything healed, I got some of my strength back, and I felt good again. However, eventually another cancer cell would pop up again, and we would start the chemo process again. With each treatment, it became more difficult to rebound. This is why the bad days are outnumbering the good days.

So my decision is not give up or quit. It is to stop treatment, heal, get my strength back, and live as many good days as possible and above all be "constructive!"

I know eventually the cancer has a good chance of returning, but we will deal with it as it comes. Hell, who knows, I may get run over tomorrow by some old person while I'm walking through the golf course parking lot!

I could say I have no regrets, but let's be honest, I believe everyone on this earth has a regret or two. That's all part of living and learning—hopefully learning from the mistakes and not repeating them. I have been fortunate to have married Debra and help raise our family, although Deb did most the raising because she was also raising me at the same time.

So there you go. We are off on the next adventure, or the fourth quarter of this game called "Life." Hopefully, it is the start of the fourth quarter and not the two-minute warning signaling the end of the game. I'll update this site after the surgery. Until then, have a Happy, Healthy and Safe New Year!

I can't thank everyone enough for all your support, love, prayers and thoughts, without it, I don't believe we could have got this far.

Free at Last, Thank GOD,
I'm Free at Last!
January 29, 2016

I'm talking about cancer—well, at least for now. We had the surgery over a week ago to have the cancer spot removed from my left lung (the only site of cancer left in my body), and all went well. When I woke up after surgery, the surgeon told me I would feel like he punched me in the chest, and the recovery would take four to six weeks. I thought, *Ha, I have been punched in the chest before, no big deal and that long to recover. Ha (again) after what I have been through, this will be child's play!*

WRONG, I woke up, and it felt like I had been pistol-whipped (I've never been pistol-whipped, but I imagine this is what it would feel like), then they took the pistol and shot me four times in the left lung (I've never been shot before, but I imagine this is what it would look and feel like to be shot). So off to the recovery race, and I feel like I tripped coming out of the gate, fell flat on my face, and nine other horses trampled over me. I am now up and running, OK walking, and I am gaining on the pack—actually, I can see the pack, barely, but I'm gaining.

They also removed the liver infusion pump during the same surgery, so I have all kinds of new scars healing, front, side, and back. I could be an attraction in a circus:

"Guess How Many Scars" or "See the Totally RIPPED Man" (at that, they would be disappointed).

We see the surgeon next Tuesday to have the stitches removed and our oncology doctor Friday to find out if it was colon cancer or lung cancer.* Not sure what the difference is, but whatever.

So, as far as I'm concerned, I'm cancer-free, and whatever 2016 brings us, we will deal with it and live life large! Deb and I hope to see everybody sometime this year. Thanks for being true friends to Deb and me throughout this two-year battle.

---

*It was determined that it was from the colon cancer, which was good. It was not a new cancer starting in the lungs.

Stoma Education!
February 28, 2016

I hadn't heard the word *stoma* until I was diagnosed with rectal colon cancer twenty-seven months ago. Then, when they told me what they were going to do to me and give a stoma that comes out the abdomen and a colostomy bag for my stoma, I said, "WHAT THE HELL ARE YOU TALKING ABOUT?" Then they calmly explained the procedure and repeated everything again, then I said, "REALLY? WHAT THE HELL ARE YOU TALKING ABOUT?"

When we got home, I looked up the word *stoma* in our *Webster's Dictionary* (remember those?), and I found nothing. So I Googled it, and I found more than I wanted to know. Whoever said "Knowledge is power" never looked up the word *stoma*.

After living for the past eighteen months with a stoma and colostomy bag, I have somewhat adjusted. It's a real lifestyle change, but you have to continually adjust and make friends with it. No, I did not give it a name, although, early on I did, but I can't repeat it in print.

So here is the education: all people and animals create gas. It is a normal, everyday thing that leads us to expel gas at one time or another throughout the day. Everybody knows this, but some don't want to admit it. Normally,

LEO DUGO

you can tell and feel when you're about to flatulate, fart, toot—whatever you want to call it. You can deal with it by excusing yourself and make a quick exit, squeeze your cheeks together to suppress it, or TALK REAL LOUD! Either way, you have some control and warning that something unpleasant is about to happen in public. In private, no big deal, let it rip. Although you still have to deal with the odor, at that time you can apologize or blame your dog or spouse, whomever you're with.

Now with a stoma, there is NO WARNING! It's proud and has NO social skills. It seems like it likes to be heard, which can be embarrassing to my wife because I always look at her and say, "Really, honey?" If I blame one of our dogs, they don't care. In fact, they look a little proud. I can squeeze my cheeks till the cows come home; it does no good. I can't make a quick exit because I didn't know it was going to happen, so I just have to bare the blame and apologize. So, if this happens in a restaurant or any public place, just remember that person may have a proud stoma they don't have any control over!

There is one advantage I do have with the colostomy bag. It has a charcoal filter that eliminates odors...now, if only it had a muffler.

We see our oncology doctor this Friday to get the latest scoop. Hope I didn't gross you out.

Ringing of "The Bell"!!!
March 4, 2016

At Siteman Cancer Center, they have a brass bell they call "The Bell." Whenever someone beats cancer and is declared cancer-free, they get to ring "The Bell" with your oncology doctor and all the oncology nurses gathered around to join in the celebration.

Today our oncology doctor, Dr. Lim, told us we are cancer-free! The scan they took two weeks ago looks like a normal person's—except it's missing some body parts and has other parts in different places, which is not normal, plus our daughters would not agree I'm normal. Anyway, we got to ring "The Bell," and what a sweet sound it was!

Our doctor said they are using my CT scans, MRIs, and PET scans as teaching and training tools. I think he was as excited as we were. Deb and I are going to kick start our life again, meaning we can make plans for up to three months at a time because that's when we go for another CT scan and doctor visit.

Thanks again from the bottom of our hearts!*

Deb and I cannot stress enough how helpful it is to have a strong support team cheering you on every step of the way. But whether you have the support of a thousand or just a few on your healthcare team, you can battle this monster and be victorious.

Ding, Ding, Ding, Round Three!
April 22, 2016

In this corner, wearing black shorts: "CANCER!" *Boo, hiss, boo!* And in this corner, wearing red, white, and blue shorts: "CANCER CLOBBERER!" *Yeah, woo-hoo!*

This is not the ringing of the bell we were looking for, but it is what it is! We feel so fortunate that I have been cancer-free for twelve weeks. I beat my old record last summer of six weeks!

No chemo since January1st has allowed my body to start the healing process and exercising to start getting my strength back. But, to be honest, deep inside, I feel this will be my new normal: chemo bout, cancer-free bout, and on it will go.

They feared because the cancer had spread to so many places, some of them would be vacationing where the chemo had not ventured and waiting until the coast was clear, signaling it was time for them to go back to work.

I had a blood test last Friday, and it showed that my tumor markers were high, although that does not mean the cancer *is* growing again; it means *maybe* it is. So today I had a PET scan to see what, if anything, was going on. We met with our oncology doctor after the PET scan and he said the cancer is back. It's a small spot in my lymph nodes, but it's back. We start chemo again next week for Round Three.

Now the good news is I'm feeling much better going into this round—not sure why, but I do. Another good thing is I'm learning to accept my stoma more. I mentioned in another journal about how difficult it is to live with a stoma because of its behavior and can be rude at the most inappropriate time. I have now come to grips that it is like having a teenager that will never leave home attached to my stomach!

We had a really good spring break, which included a road trip to Mississippi to play golf with our good friend Sue Castle, then off to Pine Mountain, GA. We stayed at Calloway Gardens and played three days of golf (Deb tortured me all three days), then off to Atlanta to see Deb's brother and visit with their families and three new grandbabies, all under two years old. Now that's a lot of babies—there's so much movement, it looked like a bucket of worms, and just watching wore us out!

Anyway, we are on to our next adventure and fight with this opponent called cancer. I'm going to the punching bag and work on my uppercut and right hook. Cancer is going DOWN! Hang in there and never give up!

Déjà Vu
May 9, 2016

Forty-one years ago, Deb was nine months pregnant with our second daughter Jessica, and I was in a body cast from the top of my head down to my hips. (Remember, the race car accident?) Obviously I was out of work because of the injury, so there we were sitting in our house, looking at each other and thinking, *Does it get any better than this?* And then Deb's water broke.

All we had was Deb's 1968 VW Bug for transportation. So off we went to the hospital, me driving (looking stiff like Herman Munster) and Deb squeezed into the shotgun seat.

Getting Deb in her pregnant state in the VW was quite a chore, I getting in the driver's seat was another story. I could bend at the hips, but absolutely no bending ability from the hips up and no peripheral vision, like Horse Blinders. To get in I had to sit on the ground and pull myself up into the seat. There we were zooming (as much zooming a 68 VW can zoom) actually just keeping up with traffic and getting some strange looks as people would pass us.

I pulled in front of the Emergency Entrance doors and they see Deb trying to extract herself from the car and they see me in a cast sitting on the ground flailing around like a fish out of water trying to stand up. They run out with 2 wheelchairs not knowing who needs help the most.

Now we are in the Maternity Room where they are seeing how close she is to delivery, which is about 30 minutes to go. All the nurses are worried about me, getting me a chair, drinks, food, blankets, etc., and every now and then check on how Deb is doing!

There was a STORM BREWING! They had to check her dilation and asked me to step out of the room, they had a chair, a drink and cookies waiting for me just outside the door. As they were checking Deb, they asked her how *I* was doing and how I got hurt.........through the closed door I heard......." "XZ@#%^ HIM, HE BROKE HIS *^$#@$ NECK IN A @#%&^*# RACE CAR, now let's get back to me! How soon will my baby girl be born?"

She was born shortly after that outburst.

Zoom forward to May 6, 2016. We were backing out of our garage, heading to the hospital because Deb was having some back issues. They would be performing a myelogram CT to find out the problem.

It hurts to walk? No big deal, WOMAN UP, woman! I'm in my second week of super-charged chemo with all the side effects kicking in, the most notable of which is the face rash that looks like I walked face first into a burning building.

I looked over at Deb and said, "Déjà vu, September 30, 1974!" We both started laughing.

When we got to the hospital, people looked at me like, *Whoa, they are going to the burn unit.* Then, while prepping Deb for the procedure, the doctor came in to explain everything. He looked at me and asked, "Whoa, severe sunburn?" *No chemo.* He asked, "What kind?" *Eight capecitabine pills a day and Irinotecan every three weeks.* He asked, "What kind of cancer?"

Meanwhile, Deb was lying there in pain and wanting the Valium to start working *NOW.* There IS A STORM BREWING, AGAIN! I looked at Deb half grinning and she said, "Back to ME, *I'm* the patient!"

We all laughed. Forty-one years ago, we didn't laugh, but we do now.

We won't have results till next week, and I start radiation in a week or so. So in a couple of weeks, we should *both* be like new.

Like Totally Rad Man!
May 22, 2016

Here is the latest: Deb has spinal stenosis again for the third time, but they feel they can control the situation with a series of shots rather than surgery. That is great news because Deb does not want another back surgery and who could blame her? Two surgeries were enough! She starts the shots June 2nd, so we are looking forward to getting her back on track and moving forward.

My daily chemo and every three weeks supercharged liquid chemo must be doing some major cancer butt kicking because all the side effects have come back with a vengeance to show me how much they missed me. Actually, I'm doing really well. When I was first diagnosed, the doctors encouraged me to keep exercising through the treatments, which I have. However, I was exercising one or two days a week, but nothing to brag about, stretch, ride the exercise bike five minutes, do one set of rubber band exercises, do one or maybe two sets of dumb bell exercises, and go eat a bowl of ice cream for my reward.

It was an effort, but not much of one. In my mind, I was doing it, and when I got tired or bored, I would lean on the "Cancer Card!" Meaning, "Well I got cancer so I probably shouldn't push it too hard, or the chemo is making me tired" or I should say *lazy*.

About a month ago, a friend of mine recommended a book called *Younger Next Year* by Chris Crowley and Henry Lodge, so I ordered it, or I should say I had our daughter Jessica order it on Amazon, beings all the bookstores closed and I can't figure out how to order books on this stupid computer. So I get this book and on the cover it says, *Live Strong, Fit, and Sexy—Until You're 80 and Beyond!"* I'm thinking *RRRRIGHT, what the hell did I just buy? I get it; my buddy Kris just pranked me, that dirty RAT!*

The more I read it, the more I got fired up and realized my "exercise program" sucked, and if I'm going to beat this thing called cancer and improve my chances of being sexy…oh, wait a minute, that ship has sailed, I mean strong and fit to survive what's ahead of me, I will need to get serious about how I exercise and eat all the right stuff.

So far so good, I have increased to four days a week and expanded my program; therefore I have been doing really well enduring this chemo treatment and will help get through a five-day radiation treatment that starts this Wednesday, May 25.

We found out this is a relatively new radiation machine called a MR Radiology, meaning the radiation is done in a MRI machine, which enables them to pinpoint the cancer cell and zap it, rather than just zap the general area, kind of a sharpshooter approach. It will be a heavier dose of radiation than I had before, but more directed toward the Bad Guy. The only downside is it will take two hours in the MRI machine; the upside is, it's only five days in a row and then I'm done.

So Deb and I are off to our new adventure of "Shots and Radical Treatment"—sounds like our younger years! Thanks for all your thoughts, notes, and prayers. If you get a chance, check that book out, I highly recommend it. Thanks, Kris, for turning me on to it.

Wild Weekend!
June 13, 2016

This last weekend was one weekend we were so looking forward to, and it was everything we had hoped for! June 12 was the St. Louis All American Soap Box Derby Race, and Truman and Remy were both racing in it. They came over one night each week in the evening for about an hour (sometimes half an hour, depending on my attention span) for the past eight weeks to assemble the cars.

Yes, they actually built the cars. Dan and I tightened everything up for safety purposes. Then they did their own car decoration and designs. Truman's was "Angry Birds" red car with Angry Bird's everywhere along with TNT boxes. Remy's was "The Polka Dot Car" white car with pink and black polka dots everywhere. Sunday, June 12th, couldn't come soon enough—for me, that is. I was like a kid waiting to run my first-ever race, couldn't sleep or eat, just wanted to get there, and go fast. OK, so you may think I was reliving my childhood through my grandchildren . . . OK, I was, you caught me.

We had to be at the race site at 7:00 am to reclaim the cars out of the impound area. To make sure we were not late, I got up at 4:30. After all, it's a 20-minute ride, but not sure what the traffic is at 6:30 am on Sunday, you know that Church traffic can be Hell!

I'll be damned, we weren't the first ones there. Their aunt Mandy made really cool team shirts with "Team Brawner" on the front and a Derby car on the back that read, "Derby Hair Don't Care." She also provided the "Motley Pit Crew" of Dylan (2001 Soap Box Winner), Weston, Bret, and Scot to do all the heavy lifting of the cars throughout the day. Huge, huge help!

Nine hours later in 93-degree heat we were done—not just done, but TOAST! It was a BLAST. Both Truman and Remy did awesome. I was so proud of how they handled themselves when they won and when they lost, my buttons were popping.

Truman drove a really good race, but ran against some really fast cars early and finished fifth. Remy raced in the final race against the car that beat Truman. If she won, she'd go on to Akron Ohio for the championship. It was an awesome race, but she was beat by two-tenths of a second and finished second! So, all in all, everyone had a great time and we finished it off with BBQ at Dan and Jessica's. What more could you ask?

I finished my five-day radiation treatment last week, but we have to wait ten weeks to see if the radiation worked. I could tell you how much fun the 90-minute MRI radiology treatment was, but I won't. I don't want to spoil all the fun for the next person. Anyway the new plan is I'm on a chemo break for the next two weeks, kind of a break, just had an infusion this morning, but I don't have to take the daily chemo pills for two weeks to let my body heal.

I get scanned in ten weeks, if I'm cancer-free, we will go a chemo maintenance program getting chemo once every three weeks to see how I handle it. If it is still there, they are talking surgery. If there are more spots showing up, they want to enroll me into an immune therapy trial that is showing great success. So whatever happens, we have a plan and we will GO FORWARD!!! Thanks for all your support; it means the world to Deb and me.

A New Hurdle
July 6, 2016

Around the first of May, I wrote about Deb having back pain, hoping it wasn't spinal stenosis. Then, after all, the test came back confirming it was severe spinal stenosis. She already had surgery for this once in 1997 and 2010 and did not want a third surgery, and who would? We went to a pain management doctor who was going to give her a series of three shots, but after the second shot without any improvement, they said she would need surgery. The surgeon who performed her previous surgeries has retired and finding a neurological surgeon who will operate on someone who has spine fusion before has been a challenge. However, we have done it, not without a lot of frustration and phone calls.

We met with the head of Washington University Neurological Surgery for an evaluation, which he confirmed the only fix is surgery, and they will help us. However, the surgery will not be performed until November. After we explained our situation, he said he would try to see what he could do to help us get in sooner, but no promises. We were grateful we have a solution to the problem and appreciate anything he can do to help us.

The LAST DANCE!
August 5, 2016

Just like Donna Summer's song "Last Dance" except this is my "Last Journal!"

We are leaving on a good note. I had my CT scan this morning and the radiation I had in June did the trick, and once again, I'm CANCER-FREE!

So now we go into the chemo maintenance mode. From here out, I will get one dose of chemo every three weeks and start the healing process and get my strength back.

Deb and I can't thank everyone enough for all the support, kind words, encouragement, and prayers you have given us. It was instrumental in helping us keep our attitude, spirits, and hope up for this thirty-two month battle. Without your support, it would have been a lot tougher hill to climb. "And that's a fact, Jack!" (Taken from the movie *Stripes*.)

Love each and every one of you!

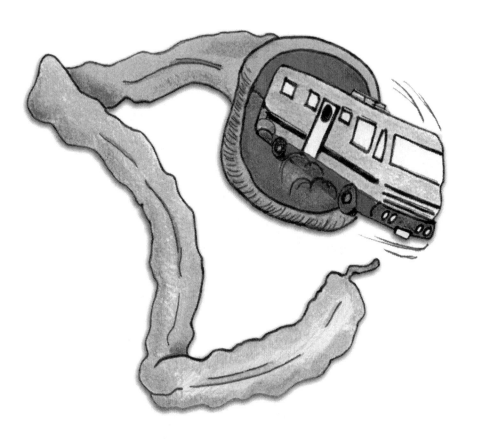

All Aboard the Colon Bus!

This illustration represents my original idea for the cover of this book. I had my cousin Jim Miller draw up my idea. Almost everybody I showed it to laughed at it, however, most of the women said it had a "Yuck factor." Jim also brought up that as a cover, this visual could limit readership to just colon cancer patients, even though this book can benefit anyone facing cancer. So with the help and suggestion of Carol and Gary Rosenberg, we chose the Roller Coaster theme. *It has been one hell of a roller coaster ride!*

CONCLUSION

We beat stage 4 colon cancer! As you can see, it was not easy, and it took a while, but in the end, it was well worth it. It is *very* important to follow *all* of your doctor's orders, prescribed treatments, exercise routines, and diet plans, but above all, maintain a good attitude and keep your faith—whatever your faith may be.

There were times I wondered, *What the hell am I doing this for?* Radiation, chemo, surgery, more radiation, and chemo? I looked around at all the wonderful things I will miss—family, friends, our dogs, golf—and decided to jump start my life again. However, it is not exactly like before. It's a new normal, which I learned to adapt to and started to enjoy life again.

There *is* life after colon cancer, and only you can decide to take the challenge of defeating this curable disease. I know my journey is not over; I'm a cancer survivor. But I'm not just surviving—I'm living life again, and Life is GOOD!

Good luck!

ACKNOWLEDGMENTS

My wife, Debra, and I would like to thank the following family, friends, and medical staff from Barnes Jewish Christian Hospital, Washington School of Medicine, and Siteman Cancer Center West for all the support, encouragement, and treatment we received throughout our journey.

Family—Jessica, Dan, Truman & Remy Brawner, Mandy Love, Dylan & Weston Price

Friends—You all know who you are; to list you all would be a book in itself!

Washington School of Medicine—Dr. Kian Lim, Dr. Matthew Silviera, Dr. Ryan Fields, Megan McDannald, Danielle Kriets, Gillian McCullough

Siteman Caner Center West—The entire staff of oncology nurses cannot be described in words! These people are heroes! The way they care for all the cancer patients is above and beyond the line of duty!

Thank you from the bottom of our hearts!

RESOURCES

Caring Bridge Website: services@caringbridge.org

Colon Cancer Support: www.ostomy.org

ABOUT THE AUTHOR

LEO DUGO worked in the construction industry in the industrial sector for forty-one years in the Midwest USA. He was born, raised, and lives in St. Louis with his wife, Debra, in the house they built themselves in 1984. They have two adult daughters, Amanda and Jessica, and four grandchildren. Leo's hobbies are woodworking and playing golf with Debra.

58355345R00083

Made in the USA
Lexington, KY
09 December 2016